HERB GARDENING
IN
TE**X**AS

THIRD EDITION

Gulf Publishing Company
Houston, Texas

SOL MELTZER

HERB GARDENING
IN
TEXAS

THIRD EDITION

With love to my wife Thelma;
to my children Melinda, John, Nancy,
and grandchildren Luken, Zachary, Sarah Grace;
and last, but not least, to my herb garden.

Herb Gardening in Texas
3rd Edition

Illustrated by Terry J. Moore

10 9 8 7 6 5 4 3 2 1

Gulf Publishing Company
Book Division
P.O. Box 2608 ☐ Houston, Texas 77252-2608

Library of Congress Cataloging-in-Publication Data
Meltzer, Sol.
    Herb gardening in Texas / Sol Meltzer. — 3rd ed.
      p.   cm.
    Includes index.
    ISBN 0-88415-329-0
    1. Herb gardening—Texas.   2. Herbs—Texas.
I. Title.
SB351.H5M358   1997
635′.7′09764—dc20   96-32644
                                      CIP

Contents

61; Herbal Dyes, 62; Reputed Herbal Medicinal Properties, 63; Herbal R_x, 65; A Word of Warning, 67

Acknowledgments

Special credits are due Taylor's Herb Garden Inc., Vista, California, for providing many of the color photographs.

Additional photo credits are due Barry Henderson, B. J. Lowe, Greg Lorfing, Marc Nekhom, Jon and Riley Newhouse, Kent Taylor, and Sol Meltzer. Gael Thompson was kind enough to do some of the drafts of my illustrations. Linda Samson deciphered my scribbling and did a fine job typing the manuscript. And thanks to Linda Mullinax and Gail Knox for additional typing. I'm grateful to Bill Adams (Harris County Extension horticulturist) for reviewing the book and, more important, for encouraging me to write it. Thanks also to Madeline Hill for her valuable criticism, and to Bill Basham of the Houston Arboretum and Botanical Gardens.

Finally, appreciation to my wife Thelma, who furnished some of the photos, read the manuscript, and supported my efforts with encouragement and constructive criticism.

Preface

Our growing conditions are completely different from those in other parts of the country. What does well in California, or up north, may not be appropriate for Texas. Many of the perennial herbs are grown as annuals in the North; in most of Texas they are perennial. Marjoram, lemon verbena, lemon grass, and rosemary are some examples. There are a few herbs, such as sweet woodruff and French tarragon, that are difficult to grow in most areas of Texas. They do well in the higher, less humid, shady areas of the state.

In Texas we have ample rain, particularly along the coast. I've taken that into consideration by suggesting soil mixtures that drain well and the use of raised beds for some herbs. I discuss and have sketches of inexpensive methods by which to propagate additional herbs from your plants. Some of the other sections cover drying and storing herbs, extracting essential oils, insecticidal properties of some of the herbs, how to make herbal insecticidal sprays, and companion plantings of herbs and vegetables to repel certain harmful insects.

With the exception of one or two, I have grown all the herbs mentioned. My herb garden is 60 by 100 feet, with approximately 100 different varieties of herbs. I wouldn't discuss certain methods of propagation, making a soil mix, growing under lights, etc., if I didn't use them myself. I consider myself a knowledgeable grower; whether I'm a worthy author is for you to judge.

Writing this book was fun. I'm sure you'll find several good ideas, have a laugh or two, and agree with me when I say that herbs make scents in Texas.

Sol Meltzer
Houston, Texas

Herb Hardiness Zone Map

The term *hardy* means the ability of a plant to survive the lowest average winter temperature for that particular zone. If (WP) follows an herb, it means winter protect in that zone. Some herbs do well in certain zones, but within that zone, variations in temperatures, rainfall, soil, etc., can mean success or failure with a particular herb. Many of the herbs, particularly the mints, may die back in zones 6, 7, and 8, but the root system remains alive and new growth is produced in the spring.

An herb listed in zone 6 is hardy in all zones. Herbs listed in zones 7 and 8 are hardy in 9 and 10 also. Those listed in zone 9 are hardy in 10.

Regardless of what zone you're in, all the herbs need to be planted early in the spring to establish a good root system for the following winter. In zones 6 and 7, herbs that need winter protection must be set out several months before the first anticipated cold weather.

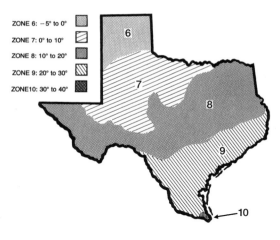

ZONE 6: −5° to 0°
ZONE 7: 0° to 10°
ZONE 8: 10° to 20°
ZONE 9: 20° to 30°
ZONE 10: 30° to 40°

Zones 6 and 7

Angelica	Mugwort
Camomile (P)	Parsley
Caraway	Pyrethrum
Catnip	Rue
Chives	Sage
Comfrey	Salad Burnet
Costmary	Santolina
Elecampane	Sassafras
Fennel (P)	Shallots
Foxglove	Southernwood
Garlic	Sweet Flag
Germander	Sweet Woodruff
Ginseng	Tansy
Horehound	Tarragon
Horseradish	Thyme
Hyssop	Watercress
Lambs Ear	Winter Savory
Lavender	Wintergreen
Lemon Balm	Wormwood
Mint	Yarrow

Zone 8

Dittany of Crete
Garlic Chives
Greek Oregano
Mexican Marigold Mint (WP)
Oregano
Pineapple Sage (WP)
Rosemary, upright
Sweet Marjoram (WP)

Zone 9

Aloe Vera (WP)
Cayenne (WP)
Ginger
Lemon Grass (WP)
Lemon Eucalyptus
Lemon Verbena (WP)
Luffa
Pennyroyal (WP)
Rosemary, prostrate (WP)
Scented Geraniums (WP)
Sweet Bay

Zone 10

Aloe Vera
Cayenne
Ginger
Lemon Grass
Lemon Verbena
Pennyroyal
Rosemary, prostrate
Scented Geraniums
Sweet Bay

Average Dates of First and Last Frosts

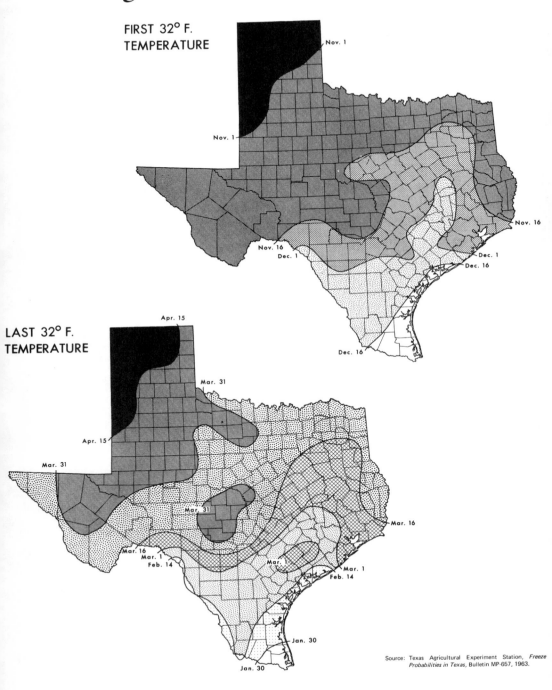

FIRST 32° F.
TEMPERATURE

Nov. 1

Nov. 1

Nov. 16

Nov. 16
Dec. 1

Dec. 1
Dec. 16

Dec. 16

LAST 32° F.
TEMPERATURE

Apr. 15

Mar. 31

Apr. 15

Mar. 31

Mar. 31

Mar. 16

Mar. 16
Mar. 1
Feb. 14

Mar. 1

Mar. 1
Feb. 14

Jan. 30

Jan. 30

Source: Texas Agricultural Experiment Station, *Freeze Probabilities in Texas*, Bulletin MP-657, 1963.

Growing Season in Texas

Station	Mean date of last spring freeze	Mean date of first fall freeze	Mean growing season	Station	Mean date of last spring freeze	Mean date of first fall freeze	Mean growing season
Abilene	Mar. 26	Nov. 12	231	Eagle Pass	Feb. 20	Dec. 3	286
Albany	Apr. 3	Nov. 5	216	Eastland	Mar. 29	Nov. 9	225
Alice	Feb. 20	Dec. 4	287	Eden	Apr. 3	Nov. 7	218
Alpine	Mar. 30	Nov. 10	225	El Campo	Feb. 17	Dec. 2	288
Amarillo	Apr. 20	Oct. 28	191	El Paso	Mar. 14	Nov. 12	243
Angleton	Mar. 2	Nov. 30	273	Encinal	Feb. 14	Dec. 8	297
Austin	Mar. 7	Nov. 22	260	Falfurrias	Feb. 10	Dec. 10	303
Ballinger	Mar. 30	Nov. 10	225	Flatonia	Mar. 4	Dec. 4	275
Balmorhea	Mar. 30	Nov. 11	226	Flint	Mar. 8	Nov. 22	259
Beaumont	Feb. 18	Nov. 24	279	Follett	Apr. 20	Oct. 28	191
Beeville	Feb. 20	Dec. 5	288	Ft. Stockton	Apr. 2	Nov. 10	222
Big Spring	Mar. 29	Nov. 11	227	Fort Worth	Mar. 20	Nov. 15	240
Blanco	Mar. 25	Nov. 3	223	Fredericksburg	Mar. 27	Nov. 3	221
Boerne	Mar. 25	Nov. 9	229	Gainesville	Mar. 29	Nov. 6	222
Bonham	Mar. 30	Nov. 7	222	Galveston	Jan. 27	Dec. 24	331
Borger	Apr. 17	Oct. 28	194	Gatesville	Mar. 24	Nov. 9	230
Brady	Mar. 29	Nov. 11	227	Goliad	Feb. 22	Dec. 1	282
Brenham	Feb. 25	Dec. 2	280	Graham	Apr. 3	Nov. 2	213
Bridgeport	Mar. 30	Nov. 5	220	Greenville	Mar. 20	Nov. 12	237
Bronson	Mar. 24	Nov. 8	229	Hallettsville	Mar. 8	Nov. 15	252
Brownsville			365	Harlingen	Jan. 24	Dec. 26	336
Brownwood	Mar. 20	Nov. 18	243	Haskell	Mar. 31	Nov. 12	226
Cameron	Mar. 15	Nov. 21	251	Henderson	Mar. 11	Nov. 13	247
Canadian	Apr. 9	Oct. 30	204	Henrietta	Mar. 28	Nov. 11	228
Canyon	Apr. 19	Oct. 28	192	Hereford	Apr. 23	Oct. 24	184
Carrizo Springs	Feb. 22	Nov. 26	277	Hico	Mar. 29	Nov. 2	218
Center	Mar. 17	Nov. 6	234	Hondo	Mar. 3	Nov. 21	263
Centerville	Mar. 14	Nov. 9	240	Houston	Feb. 4	Dec. 10	309
Childress	Apr. 1	Nov. 7	220	Huntsville	Mar. 9	Nov. 27	263
Clarksville	Mar. 30	Nov. 5	224	Iowa Park	Apr. 1	Nov. 2	215
Cleburne	Mar. 26	Nov. 10	229	Jacksboro	Apr. 2	Nov. 10	222
Coleman	Mar. 28	Nov. 5	222	Junction	Apr. 2	Nov. 2	214
College Station	Mar. 6	Nov. 27	266	Karnack	Mar. 18	Nov. 4	231
Colorado City	Apr. 5	Nov. 3	212	Kaufman	Mar. 21	Nov. 15	239
Conroe	Mar. 6	Nov. 23	262	Kenedy	Mar. 5	Nov. 26	266
Corpus Christi	Feb. 9	Dec. 12	306	Kerrville	Apr. 4	Nov. 6	216
Corsicana	Mar. 13	Nov. 20	252	Kirbyville	Mar. 22	Nov. 7	230
Cotulla	Feb. 24	Nov. 25	274	Knox City	Apr. 1	Nov. 9	222
Crockett	Mar. 16	Nov. 9	238	Lampasas	Mar. 30	Nov. 8	223
Crosbyton	Apr. 11	Nov. 2	205	Laredo	Jan. 31	Dec. 19	322
Crystal City	Mar. 2	Nov. 27	270	Levelland	Apr. 13	Oct. 30	200
Cuero	Mar. 8	Nov. 27	264	Liberty	Mar. 1	Nov. 15	259
Dalhart	Apr. 23	Oct. 25	185	Lindale	Mar. 12	Nov. 11	244
Dallas	Mar. 18	Nov. 12	239	Livingston	Mar. 14	Nov. 17	248
Danevang	Feb. 23	Dec. 5	285	Llano	Mar. 27	Nov. 10	228
Del Rio	Feb. 10	Dec. 10	303	Longview	Mar. 15	Nov. 12	242
Denison Dam	Mar. 26	Nov. 10	229	Lubbock	Apr. 11	Nov. 1	204
Dilley	Feb. 25	Dec. 2	280	Lufkin	Mar. 18	Nov. 4	231
Dublin	Mar. 26	Nov. 17	236	Luling	Mar. 3	Nov. 24	266

Table continued on next page.

Table continued from previous page.

Station	Mean date of last spring freeze	Mean date of first fall freeze	Mean growing season	Station	Mean date of last spring freeze	Mean date of first fall freeze	Mean growing season
Madisonville	Mar. 9	Nov. 12	248	Rio Grande City	Feb. 11	Dec. 13	305
Marathon	Apr. 5	Nov. 1	210	Rising Star	Mar. 28	Nov. 6	223
Marshall	Mar. 14	Nov. 13	244	Rocksprings	Mar. 28	Nov. 17	234
Matagorda	Feb. 13	Dec. 14	304	Roscoe	Apr. 6	Nov. 6	214
Maurbo	Feb. 23	Dec. 2	282	Rusk	Mar. 16	Nov. 8	237
McAllen	Jan. 30	Dec. 10	314	San Angelo	Mar. 25	Nov. 13	233
McCamey	Mar. 26	Nov. 11	230	San Antonio	Mar. 3	Nov. 26	268
McCook	Feb. 5	Dec. 8	306	San Benito	Jan. 13	Dec. 26	347
McKinney	Apr. 1	Nov. 5	218	San Marcos	Mar. 13	Nov. 19	251
Memphis	Apr. 5	Nov. 2	211	Sealy	Feb. 27	Dec. 2	278
Mexia	Mar. 16	Nov. 21	250	Seminole	Apr. 10	Nov. 2	206
Miami	Apr. 19	Oct. 23	187	Seymour	Apr. 4	Oct. 31	210
Midland	Mar. 28	Nov. 15	232	Sherman	Mar. 20	Nov. 7	232
Mineral Wells	Mar. 25	Nov. 6	226	Smithville	Mar. 11	Nov. 15	249
Mission	Jan. 26	Dec. 18	326	Snyder	Apr. 5	Nov. 4	213
Montague	Mar. 29	Nov. 6	222	Spearman	Apr. 22	Oct. 24	185
Mount Locke	Apr. 23	Oct. 26	186	Spur	Apr. 17	Oct. 28	194
Mount Pleasant	Mar. 25	Nov. 9	229	Sugar Land	Feb. 14	Nov. 29	288
Muleshoe	Apr. 20	Oct. 20	183	Sulphur Springs	Mar. 24	Nov. 3	224
Munday	Apr. 6	Nov. 7	215	Tahoka	Apr. 6	Nov. 5	213
Nacogdoches	Mar. 16	Nov. 10	239	Taylor	Mar. 14	Nov. 18	249
New Braunfels	Mar. 11	Nov. 26	260	Temple	Mar. 10	Nov. 24	259
Palacios	Feb. 12	Dec. 4	295	Throckmorton	Apr. 4	Nov. 7	217
Palestine	Mar. 14	Nov. 15	246	Uvalde	Mar. 9	Nov. 18	254
Paris	Mar. 27	Nov. 10	228	Van Horn	Mar. 31	Nov. 5	219
Pecos	Mar. 31	Nov. 8	222	Vega	Apr. 21	Oct. 21	183
Pierce	Mar. 6	Nov. 27	266	Victoria	Feb. 6	Dec. 8	305
Plainview	Apr. 11	Nov. 4	207	Waco	Mar. 16	Nov. 18	247
Port Arthur	Jan. 30	Dec. 8	312	Waxahachie	Mar. 25	Nov. 5	225
Port Isabel			365	Weatherford	Mar. 28	Nov. 7	224
Port Lavaca	Feb. 18	Dec. 8	293	Weslaco	Jan. 22	Dec. 13	325
Port O'Connor	Feb. 6	Dec. 20	317	Whitney Dam	Mar. 18	Nov. 10	237
Poteet	Mar. 6	Nov. 19	258	Wichita Falls	Apr. 4	Nov. 6	216
Presidio	Mar. 18	Nov. 13	240	Wink	Mar. 26	Nov. 9	228
Quanah	Apr. 3	Nov. 4	215	Ysleta	Apr. 3	Nov. 1	212
Raymondville	Jan. 25	Dec. 22	331				

Source: U.S. Department of Commerce, Climates of the States, Texas.

Herbs: Mysterious, Medicinal & Marvelous

To a botanist, a herb, or an "erb" (either pronunciation is correct), is a plant that does not develop a woody stem and whose leaves and stem die down entirely sometime after flowering. Herbs may be annual, biennial, or perennial. To most people, the name *herb* refers to plants, shrubs, and even some trees, whose leaves, flowers, seeds, and other parts are used for flavoring, fragrance, or medicinal purposes. It's a very general classification, and in this book I've taken the liberty of incorporating some trees that I've never seen classified as herbs.

The terms *spices* and *herbs* mean the same to many people. I prefer to classify spices as pungent or aromatic products derived from the bark, roots, fruit, or berries of certain vegetable plants, including cinnamon, ginger, nutmeg, and sassafras among others. Sassafras is both an herb and a spice, for the roots and young shoots make a tea and the leaves are used to thicken gumbo.

Most of the familiar herbs are native to the Mediterranean area, but some are native to North and South America.

Historically, the most important use of herbs was medicinal. The study and use of herbs dates back well over 5,000 years to the Sumerians, who described uses for laurel, thyme, and many other herbs. Over 2,500 years ago the Chinese had an herb book that described over 300 medicinal plants and ways to use them. The Egyptians used many herbs, too. Some of their

1

People have grown, studied, and used herbs for over 5,000 years. Pictured here are costmary (left), hyssop (center), peppermint (bottom), and French thyme (right.)

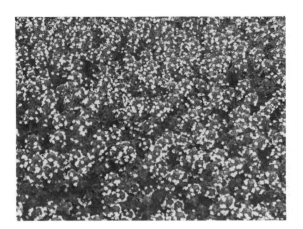

favorites were garlic, coriander, the mints, and indigo (the latter for dyeing their cloth). Both the Old and New Testaments of the Bible contain numerous references to herbs.

In the fourth century B.C. the first book on botany, *Historia Plantarum,* was complied by the Greek botanist Theophrastus. The first book on herbs by a European, describing over 500 plants, was written by a Greek physician, Discorides, in the first century A.D.

From early in the fourth century through the Middle Ages, the monasteries became the hub of herb gardening, dispensing many medicinal herbs. The monks also preserved and updated all the herbal manuscripts.

The best known herbals (writings about herbs) in English were *The Herball,* by John Gerard in about 1600, and the *English Physician Enlarged* by Nicholas Culpeper in about 1650. Culpeper's book combined herb uses, folklore, medicine, astrology, and magic. It was a number one book in those days, and it's still a good one today.

Years ago, if an herb looked like a part of the human anatomy or organ, it was assumed that it had medicinal value for that part. The leaves of lungwort, for example, were taken to resemble diseased lungs and so were thought to cure chest ailments and breathing difficulties. I have several books on herb potions and remedies in vogue three to four centuries ago. Some of these concoctions appear on pages 65–66.

Yet, many herbs *are* important sources of medicine: Foxglove yields digitalis, a heart stimulant. *Rauwolfia serpentina* from India is a source of the tranquilizer reserpine; morphine is a sedative derived from the opium poppy; quinine comes from cinchona bark; and curare, from South America, is a poison that is used as a muscle relaxant. And one we are all familiar with is the aloe vera leaf, which is very beneficial for burns, sunburn, minor cuts, bruises, and abrasions.

Herb Gardens

Herb gardens have a peculiar charm. Many of the plants have an almost fairy-tale appearance. Walking through an herb garden, with its exotic fragrances and rainbow colors, can really be a spiritual experience. Some people think of herbs as dull, green, unattractive plants. But just explore an herb garden; you'll find it a sensual delight. And there is entertaining diversity in plant characteristics: leaf colors range from the gilt of variegated golden mint to the gray-greens of lavender and wormwood; the greens are exquisite—parsley is a soft green, while pineapple sage is a rich, dark green. Interplant these two for a lush, verdant effect. Leaf textures are quite varied—lamb's ear, with its soft, furry leaves, makes a striking contrast to the coarse leaves of comfrey and borage. Your herb garden can be redolent with many unusual and delightful fragrances, from lemon verbena to peppermint-scented geranium.

Herbs make practical and versatile gardens. They can be planted as formal or informal gardens, in a rock garden, as ground covers, or as a culinary garden. These are just a few possibilities to stir your imagination. There are many situations for an herb garden—as many as you can imagine.

When most herbs reach half their mature size, they aren't bothered by the bugs. Fertilizing requirements are minimal; a light application of fertilizer after pruning is all that is necessary. The mints require additional watering, but most herbs manage very well with minimum water.

Informal plantings require less care than a formal garden. Both types of gardens have their place around the home. A delicate border of moss-curled parsley, with its lovely shades of soft green, is both practical and decorative. Compact green bush basil reaches a height of 8 or 10 inches and makes an excellent low border plant along a walk or driveway. Its natural compact shape makes pruning unnecessary. Some of the dwarf varieties of opal basil are a few inches taller than the compact green basil. A planting of both opal and green basil makes a striking color combination. My variegated opal basil has an unusual color variation, with variegated purple and green leaves. I grew it from seeds I collected from my green and opal basil, which had grown side by side and cross-pollinated. Grow some green and opal basil yourself, collect the seeds, and see what happens when you plant them in the spring.

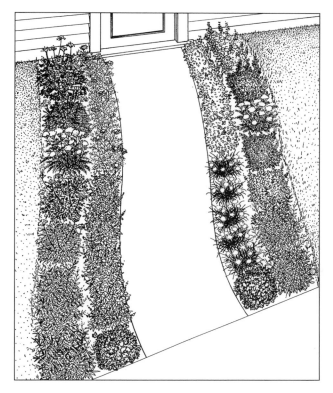

Herbs planted along the walk from the house to the driveway make leaving and returning home a little more interesting. Outer left row (from back): coriander, anise, yarrow, coriander, anise, and lemon verbena. Inner left row: English camomile, Corsican mint, and curled parsley. Outer right row: wintergreen, sweet marjoram, yarrow, sweet marjoram, wintergreen, and lemon verbena. Inner right row: pennyroyal, chives, and curled parsley.

Common thyme, with its small gray-green leaf and delicate small white flowers, makes a fine low hedge along a driveway or walk. Thyme may require a little pruning for shape. Silver, green, and lemon thyme make an unusual hedge or edge border.

I have several germanders randomly planted in my garden. The plants are 1 foot high and 2 feet wide, with small waxy green leaves similar to oak leaves and make a lovely hedge. The flowers bloom for several weeks and are a beautiful salmon color. Prostrate rosemary, hardy in Zones 9 and 10, has delicate blue flowers and is a most attractive, unusual low hedge. Don't prune any hedges until after they flower or you'll miss a good part of their beauty. Prostrate rosemary plants should be spaced 18 inches apart for a nice tight hedge and 4 feet apart if you want to interplant with other herbs. They flower from late May to July, depending on what zone you're in. Lavender is also a striking border, with its soft gray foliage and delicate blue blossoms.

A combination of hyssop and rue, two more herbs less than 2 feet tall, makes an unusual hedge. There are three varieties of hyssop: white, blue, and pink. Rue has blue-gray leaves and small yellow flowers that make a sharp contrast when interplanted with hyssop. Chives form lovely lilac-colored seed heads and are great borders for your herb bed. Try interplanting these with garlic chives, which have pretty white flowers and are in perfect contrast to the flowering chives.

Several of the thymes are well adapted to rock garden culture. Mother of thyme (creeping thyme) fills the rock crevices and spills out over the rocks. Caraway-scented thyme, with its pink flowers, is lovely interplanted among unusual rocks. Prostrate rosemary, lemon, silver, and garden thyme blend very well in the rock garden. The compact bush basils (opal and green) are two more herbs to interplant.

Camomile and pennyroyal make excellent ground covers. Pennyroyal will cover a large area in one growing season. Sweet woodruff, another ground cover, needs lots of shade. It does best in the eastern portions of Zones 7 and 8.

Most of the herbs make unusual individual plantings. The santolinas, gray or green, are coral-like in appearance and require very little care. They reach up to 3 feet across and 1 foot tall.

Scatter larger herbs throughout the garden or as plantings around your home. Pineapple sage reaches 4 feet across and has lovely little red flowers that cover most of the bush during the summer. Mexican marigold mint has yellow button-like flowers and makes a fine planting against the house or as an individual plant. Catnip and lemon balm can get out of hand and need pruning to keep them in bounds. Upright rosemary, which reaches a height of 3 feet, is great in combination with golden and variegated sage.

White yarrow, with its fern-like leaves and large white flower head, is an asset in any garden. The pink variety is smaller than the white, the yellow variety is taller. White yarrow can cover a large growing area during one growing season. It does not require any care, but by midsummer you'll need to cut back on the size of the bed so that it doesn't take over the entire garden.

Many herbs are excellent for rock gardens. Formal plantings like these always arouse interest and add an elegant touch to the landscape. The herbs illustrated here are all sandy soil plants and will tolerate a partial-to-full sun exposure. From front: creeping thyme spills out over rocks, hyssop, lavender, dittany of Crete, sage, English camomile, santolina, garlic, and pineapple sage.

Want to bring bees around to help pollinate your growing plants? Bees like lemon balm, borage, marjoram, thyme, lavender, hyssop, and many more.

You don't need a large culinary herb garden to supply herbs for flavoring. A 4- by 8-foot garden near your back door will easily manage a few basil, three or four shallot clumps, two clumps of chives, three or four summer savory, a restricted mint bed, a few parsley and one each of tarragon, rosemary, sage, marjoram, and thyme. Scatter some dill seeds throughout the garden and thin to a dozen plants. Dill reaches a height of 4 feet and does well among the other herbs.

Formal herb gardens require more attention than informal ones. There are unlimited shapes and sizes for a formal garden. You can design one for a triangle, square, circle, half circle, etc. You may want to close it in with a hedge of rosemary, santolina, pineapple sage, lavender, or germander. You can plant sections of herbs with the same shades of green or gray. A formal garden planted around a sundial with spokes of scented geraniums radiating out from the center is quite impressive. A design like this also offers many possibilities for herb combinations. Plan your formal garden, allocating space for the herbs you wish to plant (see the chart on pages 183–186). Should you incorporate mint, remember to restrict the root system (otherwise, mint can take over the whole garden). If your garden is suitable for a ground cover, try dittany of Crete—its foliage forms a thick mat of leaves and does well in sunny locations. Woolly thyme is another excellent ground cover. Remember to keep your tall herbs in the back of your garden; smaller herbs that require some shade can be planted in front of the tall ones. Check the chart on pages 183–186 for herb sizes and plan your formal garden accordingly.

Growing Herbs in Texas

Most of the herb books in my library are slanted to growing either on the West Coast or in the North and Northeast. Texas has different growing conditions, requirements, and insects larger and more destructive than in other parts of the country. We have a longer growing season, and herbs grown as annuals up north are perennial here in Texas. Rosemary, marjoram, sweet bay, lemon verbena, and other tender perennials can be grown outdoors all year in most of Texas. Some need winter protection such as a mulch, or, if a hard freeze is predicted, a substantial cover. A few of the herbs are difficult to grow, especially along the Gulf Coast. French tarragon and sweet woodruff, for example, need shade as well as cooler weather than our 90° plus.

Most herbs are natives of the Mediterranean, and because of this several authors have described them as growing best in poor soil and in full sun, which helps them generate their essential oils. These authors also write that too much water, fertilizer, and shade results in herbs with less oil but lush foilage. However, it has been my experience that few of the herbs will survive in poor soil. I don't recommend a regular program of fertilizing and watering your herb plants, but they do need some attention.

I'm sure that the herb seeds we purchase or collect are quite different in culture from their Mediterranean ancestors. Their growing requirements have changed considerably over the years. Several of the herbs requiring minimum water include lavender, sage, santolina, thyme, and rosemary.

Herbs are fun to grow. Start off with half a dozen, either from seeds or live plants, and keep adding new ones.

All the annuals and most of the perennials are started from seed; parsley, sage, marjoram, chives, basil, dill, and thyme are examples. Nurseries throughout Texas usually have a good selection of herb seeds and plants. If you can't find what you want, check the section on "Sources" (page 189) for seed companies from which you can mail-order herb seeds and/or plants.

Live plants that are mail-ordered are smaller than those purchased locally. In a short period of time, and with minimum care, the plant will be vigorous and healthy. Before you order live plants, check with your friends and neighbors—they may have herbs from which you can take cuttings.

Propagating herbs from cuttings is easy. (See pages 23–26 for details.) In three to four weeks, most of the cuttings develop vigorous root systems and are suitable for potting. It doesn't hurt a plant when you take cuttings; it is beneficial—proper pruning stimulates additional growth.

Getting Started

Some herbs to purchase as starter plants or propagate from cuttings are sweet bay, comfrey, costmary, French tarragon, lemon grass, lemon verbena, scented geraniums (some seeds are available), rosemary (seeds are slow germinating), southernwood, unusual thymes (lemon, golden, silver, etc.), wormwood, and yarrow. The other herbs can be grown from seed (for details on seed propagation see pages 20–23).

Plant seeds directly in the garden or start them indoors, whichever you prefer. I recommend starting lavender seeds indoors; I've never had much luck with them outside. Until recently, I wasn't successful indoors or out with lavender seeds. A friend grew some for me and showed me how: Plant the seeds in a container of moist vermiculite, barely covering the seed. You can keep the container on a window sill and the seeds will sprout in 10 to 20 days. Although it is usually recommended that you wait until the seedlings have at least four leaves before transplanting to individual containers, if you are as impatient as I am, with a little care you can transplant when the seedlings have a pair of leaves. I have grown and transplanted thousands of seedlings with one set of leaves and have lost very few.

Remember, any time you set out a plant in your garden, whether the plant was purchased from a nursery, mail-ordered, or even one you've grown indoors, transplanting is going to shock it. But, though it has been grown in a controlled environment, it can easily be adapted to its new home. In cool weather this isn't much of a problem. When the weather is warm, transplant late in the day, water well, and mulch. Put a box, a piece of cardboard, or any container on the west side of the plant to provide some shade. You may see some wilt the first few days. If you do, spray the leaves with water a few times a day. You can plant herbs or any plant during hot weather if you'll water, mulch, and provide shade for a few days.

Hotcaps, fabricated from anything handy, help protect new transplants from the strong summer sun. New plants may wilt the first few days; if they do, spray with water several times a day.

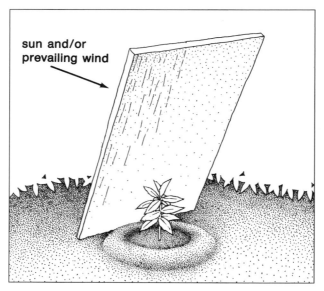

Another simple way to protect transplants: Stick a piece of cardboard or wood in the direction of the sun and/or prevailing wind.

A Little Pruning Helps

As your herbs grow and the weather gets hot, some, such as catnip, lemon balm, and particularly the mints, will tend to get scraggly. Don't hesitate to prune—even severely. I have some large mint beds and prune several times a year with my lawnmower. People come from miles away to smell my mint-scented lawnmower! Pruning (it's not necessary to use a lawnmower) encourages new growth that results in bushier plants. You can extend the life of some of your annuals by continual light pruning to keep them from flowering. When annuals flower and set seed, they've reached the end of their life cycle. My wife has a few sweet basil plants outside the back door that she uses for cooking. She keeps them well pruned, and her plants last much longer than the ones I have out in my garden and don't prune.

Many of the annuals and perennials will drop seed. I have volunteer seedlings of basil, catnip, lemon balm, and dill scattered throughout the garden. Here in Houston I haven't had to plant dill in a few years. I've seen dill make it through winters as cold as 12°.

A Few Things to Remember, and a Few You Should Try

Plan your plantings by checking the chart (pages 183–186) to see how large the herbs will be at maturity. If your herb is a perennial, plant in an area where it will enjoy living for several years.

Comfrey and horseradish should be off in a corner of the garden. Horseradish roots reach a considerable distance horizontally and vertically. When you harvest the roots, it's difficult to dig up every bit of root, and even a small piece of root means another plant. Comfrey roots do not have the range of horseradish roots, but they can be a problem if you don't dig up every piece.

I'm assuming that everyone has a garden with plenty of room for herbs, but you *don't* need a lot of growing space. Herbs can be tucked in among your bushes, flowers, and vegetables. Perhaps you live in an apartment and don't have a garden: containers and hanging baskets of herbs do very well on the patio. Even if all you have is a sunny window, you can still grow quite a few varieties. If you live in a closet, herbs do great under gro-lights.

In fact, I grow quite a few herb seedlings under lights in my garage, which is offset from my home and backs up to a large field. One year when my basil was a few inches high, the field mice got into the garage and cleaned me out. But I found a great deterrent: a cat!

Herbs do well as border plants. A row of flowering chives adds beauty to the yard. The bush, opal, and sacred basils are unusual and striking border plants. A permanent low hedge of prostrate and upright rosemary is lovely. Germander, lavender, winter savory and many others also make lovely hedges. In Zones 9 and 10, rosemary can be planted directly in the ground. It should be planted in early spring so it will develop a good root system before the first freeze. In other zones, large pots of rosemary can be buried in the ground. They should be brought indoors before the first freeze, though.

Insects attack many of the herbs, but damage is minimal. It's different when a vegetable plant is attacked by insects: if the fruit is severely damaged, the plant is of little value. With most herbs the leaf is usually the flavoring portion. If there are a few holes in some of the leaves, or if several are totally destroyed, it's no real problem. Young basil plants are chewed on, and so is sage. The mints also get their share of gnawing. Red spiders like rosemary in containers but don't seem to care for it out of the garden.

Many of the herbs have natural insecticidal properties and attract harmful insects away from vegetables and onto themselves. The odor of some herbs actually deters some destructive insects: garlic repels aphids, and French marigold exudes a natural chemical that kills or repels some nematodes. This eel-like worm attacks the roots of tomato plants and many other vegetables. Marigolds planted around your tomato plants will help eliminate this pest. Nasturtiums repel the squash bug. Companion-planting vegetables and herbs is something I've done for years. (Charts on companion plantings of herbs and vegetables, and herbs that repel insects, appear on pages 57–58.)

Grow Your Own

Although seeds are not expensive, it's fun to collect your own. If you're growing several varieties of herbs, collecting for next year will mean a savings. The basils are easy to collect. When the long seed pod turns brown, collect and store in a large sack in a dry place. In about a month, you can screen the seeds through a household kitchen strainer. Seeds should be stored in a dry cool area in metal or plastic containers. Bugs and mice will chew through paper envelopes. I mention basil, but most herbs seeds are easy to collect. They are all gathered in the same manner. Dill is a bit different. Cut the seed head when it first turns brown. If you let the seeds completely dry on the plant, the wind will blow most of them away.

Soil

If you are one of the fortunate few who have excellent soil, skip this part of the chapter. If your soil can be improved, keep reading. Most herbs do well in average garden soil. If you have a heavy soil, I suggest that you work in some sand to improve porosity and permeability. What are porosity and permeability? A sponge has holes throughout; the holes mean the sponge is porous. If all these holes are interconnected, it is permeable. Porous, permeable soil can absorb large quantities of water, releasing it slowly to plant roots; this also allows better air circulation for the roots of growing plants, which encourages root extension, increasing the plant's feeding area and providing additional moisture when needed.

Potting Mix for Container Herbs

You can buy good potting soil mixtures, and I would suggest doing this for a few small containers. But if you plan to grow more than a few herbs, and especially if you'll be using larger containers, here's a mixture you can make for a fourth of the retail cost. To 8 parts of screened soil add 2 parts of sharp sand, 2 parts of moistened peat moss, 2 parts of perlite or vermiculite, and 1 part of screened compost or composted cow manure. These materials should be mixed thoroughly. If you have sandy soil, exclude the sand from the mix. The soil in my area is tight and heavy, and I have had good results for the past several years with the soil mix I'm recommending. With this mix, you may want to vary some of the proportions of the different materials. Use a mixture that meets the needs in your particular area.

If your soil is tight and heavy, add some sand to improve porosity and permeability.

Screen soil for potted plants prior to sowing seed. This makes the soil friable and helps the seedling root easier.

Several commercial soilless mixtures are available. I use a product called Redi-Earth. It is a mixture of vermiculite, peat moss, and minerals. Although it's best to use your own mix for containers that are gallon-size and larger, the commercial mix is great for smaller containers because it works well and is easy to mix up. I pour the mix into a large, clean garbage can, add water and mix throughly until it's the consistency of mud. A large quantity can be mixed up in a few minutes. There are enough nutrients in a 3-inch pot of this mix to sustain an herb for approximately 30 days, and because the mix retains water well, the plants require less watering in hot weather. It is an excellent growing medium and helps plants develop good root systems in a short time. It's more expensive than my own mix, but it's worth it.

Compost

The greatest additive for your soil is compost. Heavy clay soils are made fluffy and porous by incorporating large amounts of compost. It also adds "body" to sandy soils, increasing their capacity to hold moisture. Compost is the most complete and natural fertilizer.

Compost, in its simplest form, amounts to piling up refuse, allowing it to decompose for six months to a year, and then incorporating it into the soil. I have made compost for years, and it's neither difficult nor expensive.

A compost pile should be 3 to 4 feet wide, 5 feet high, and as long as you want it to be. It can be closed in with cinder blocks, a wire enclosure, a pit can be dug (that's tough work) or simply layered material on the surface (dig up the sod first) as I do. Any and all organic materials can go into the compost. Materials available in Texas include all your garbage (no bones, meat, or fat), seaweed (rich in the trace elements), grass cuttings that your neighbors set out in neat plastic bags for you; leaves and pine needles (also rich in trace elements); manure from horses, cattle, poultry, pigs and rabbits; rice hulls, peanut shells, cotton seed hulls, sawdust, weeds, wood ashes from your fireplace (rich in potash), hay and straw. If you're a fisherman, fish scraps and shrimp waste contains many of the trace elements. I carry several plastic bags with me when I'm at the beach or in the woods and bring back many treasures for the compost pile.

A good mix of table scraps (excluding meat, bones, and fat) will assure inclusion of calcium, magnesium, iron, boron, copper, zinc, etc. I add green sand or granite dust for potash and rock phosphate for phosphorus. Rock phosphate contains many valuable trace elements, including calcium, iron, boron, and iodine. Fifty-pound sacks of these fertilizers can be purchased at local nurseries and stores specializing in organic gardening supplies. Before

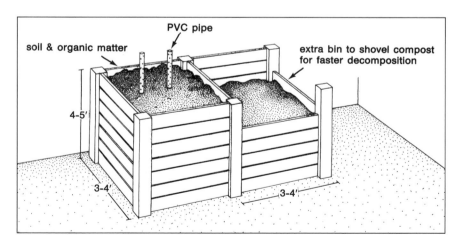

Your compost pile should be 3 to 4' wide, 5' high, and as long as you like. Perforated PVC pipe inserted into the pile will help furnish oxygen, which speeds up decomposition and reduces the strong odor.

I discuss building the compost, which can be done anytime of year, let's look at the basics.

- *The proper proportion of raw materials.* If you have enough garbage and/or grass clippings, you may not need manure, fresh or composted, to supply the necessary nitrogen. The nitrogen furnishes the heat to break down and literally cook the material.
- *The particles should be about an inch in size.* If they are larger, it slows the process. If the particles are too fine, they can solidify and not much will happen. Your lawnmower can be used for chopping up some of the materials.
- *Proper dimensions.* The compost pile should be 3 to 4 feet wide, 4 to 5 feet high, and as long as you care to make it.
- *Proper moisture and air.* These are absolute necessities. The consistency of a wet sponge squeezed out describes the proper moisture content. Heavy wire set on a few bricks, as a base for your compost, will provide a good source of air. A few 2 × 4s or a couple of pipes set into the pile and pulled out when it reaches proper height will also furnish air to the organic furnace.

Layers of alternate material should be 2 to 4 inches thick of garbage, grass cuttings, manure, and whatever you have on hand. It may take you a few weeks to reach the proper size. Wet each layer as you add to the pile. Never, I mean *never* end up with garbage on top. You'll attract every critter in the neighborhood. To avoid this, some gardeners keep the completed pile covered with black plastic until it is composted.

With proper material, particle size, moisture, air, and pile size, the compost will heat up to 160° in a few days. My compost may take six months to decompose since I rarely turn the pile. It can be made in two to three weeks by turning every three to four days to bring the finished material from the center to the outside and vice-versa. When the compost cools enough, you'll probably see a number of worms. They help compost the pile and are beneficial to the soil.

Finished compost is sweet-smelling, spongy, dark brown material and much of what you used is probably recognizable. The compost is as rich in nutrients as the variety of the raw materials used. Compost will improve the texture, porosity and permeability of the soil and its rich nutrients will be released very slowly to the plants. In heavy soils, compost improves friability and allows water to penetrate better. In light sandy soils, it works the other way, making them spongier and better able to retain moisture.

When your compost pile is finished, mix it into the top 4 inches of your soil. By itself, it's a bit rich to grow herbs.

Some manufacturers claim compost "activators" will hasten the breakdown of organic material. In a number of carefully controlled tests by the University of California, assorted compost activators were added to raw material in the recommended amounts with no observable effects. Those piles that were injected decomposed no faster than piles without activators.

A word of caution on grass clippings: don't pile them in a large heap or load up your garbage can with them and forget about it. A study by the Health Department of Santa Clara County, California, found that there are as many as 3,000 house fly larvae (maggots) in one pint of decomposing grass. If you don't compost your grass clippings, you can use them as a mulch for your herbs, trees, and shrubs. An inch-thick layer of grass will dry very quickly. You can add to the mulch when additional clippings are available. They will decompose, enrich the soil, help retain moisture. As a result, mulched areas require less watering. Mulching is excellent for everything that grows: herbs, flowers, shrubs, vegetable gardens, and trees.

I don't think there is a homeowner in Texas who needs to set out grass clippings for the local sanitation department to pick up. They can be put to good use right in your own yard. It amuses me to see all those sacks of grass set out on the curb to be taken away (I wind up with most of them). The next day, here comes the man from the local nursery with sacks of commercial fertilizer that probably cost several dollars per sack and have the same nutrients as the clippings the garbage man picked up yesterday.

Propagating the Herbs

There are several ways to propagate herbs. The most common practice is to plant seeds directly in the ground. Herbs can also be grown from seed indoors and, when the seedlings are large enough, transplanted to the garden. Cuttings from the herbs can be rooted in a rooting medium just as you'd do with ornamentals. Another technique is plant division, or propagation from a piece of root. The slowest method, and that which requires the least care, is ground or air layering.

Seeds

Most of the herbs—annual, biennial, and perennial—can be grown from seed. In the spring, the seeds can be sown in the garden. In two to three weeks, with adequate moisture and warm weather, the seedlings will sprout. When they're a few inches tall, thin out plants to the proper spacing for mature plants (see the chart on pages 183–186). Surplus plants can be transplanted to other growing areas. This works fine for basil, savory, dill, and a few other herbs. But I recommend starting most of your herb seedlings indoors and transplanting when plants are large enough and the weather is mild.

Seeds can be started either in a sterile soil mix, a commercial soilless mix, or vermiculite or perlite. If you use vermiculite or perlite, the sprouted seedlings need to be fertilized weekly. Use a good all-purpose fertilizer (I use a fish emulsion) for any plant.

The soil mix as described on pages 14–16 should be screened and sterilized prior to seeding. Soil can be sterilized by baking in the oven (a shallow cake pan is fine) at 200° for an hour. When the soil is cool, the seeds can be sown. Perlite and vermiculite are sterile; if you start seeds in either of these, the oven cycle is not necessary.

(1) Place seeds in styrofoam cups with holes punctured in the bottom for drainage, then place cups in a tray of water and let them soak; seal off the tray in a plastic bag.

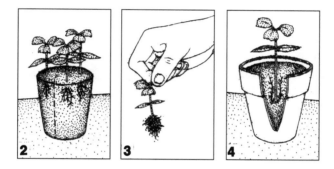

*(2) When the first set of true leaves appears, tap the soil out of the container and gently pick up all of the seedlings, grasping them by the leaves, not the roots (3); (4) when transplanting each seedling to its own pot, be sure to **avoid** jamming the roots in an upright position, as shown.*

When seeds are planted directly in the ground, the sun's rays neutralize all of the harmful soil bacteria. If unsterilized soil is used for growing seeds indoors, however, seeds as well as young seedlings can experience damping-off. Some of the seeds won't sprout, and when seedlings are a few inches tall, fungi attack the tender stems at the soil level and they literally keel over.

Any kind of container that provides adequate drainage can be used to grow seeds. The clear plastic shoe boxes you get at most of the discount stores make excellent containers. The shoe box does not have drainage, but minimum-size 3-inch containers can be filled with soil and seeded and will do beautifully in this plastic greenhouse.

Fill the clean containers with soil or growing medium and soak thoroughly, allowing the excess moisture to drain off. Plant the seeds; if they're small, press firmly into the soil. The bottom of an extra container works very well for tamping the seeds. Larger seeds should be covered with moist soil and tamped down. A good rule of thumb for planting seeds is to cover the seed with an amount of soil three times the diameter of the seed. Thus, if the seed is ⅛ of an inch in diameter, cover with an inch of soil. If you plant your seeds at the proper depth, you'll find that germination percent increases appreciably.

Each container of seeds in the shoe box greenhouse should be labeled with date and the plant variety. Put the top on, and in seven to ten days most herb seeds will sprout. This little greenhouse can be set on a windowsill, on a table, or anyplace, for it doesn't need sun. It must, however, be inspected daily. When the first green sprouts appear, place the box in a sunny location. The best growing environment would be under grolux lights for 12–14 hours a day.

It isn't necessary to remove the cover until the seedlings almost touch the top. When the top is removed, the seedlings should not be watered for a few days. Watering is one of the main determinants of success or failure with seeds and seedlings. The soil should be moist but not wet when the seeds are planted. A temperature of about 75° should also be maintained. The small greenhouse will maintain both conditions during the germination period; as the seedlings grow, you'll have to moisten the soil slightly. Small plants dry out very quickly, and young seedlings can be lost. Plant roots must have air as well as water, so, if the soil is kept too wet, the plant can die. On bright sunny days, you may need to water the plants a few times; on cloudy days perhaps not at all. When the seedlings are large enough, with two or four leaves, they can be planted in individual containers.

Removing the seedlings and soil from the container is a simple matter. Turn the pot on its side, hold it in one hand and tap the bottom sharply with the palm of the other hand. This should be done over some paper. Gently pick apart each seedling, retaining some soil around the roots. Plant each seedling slightly deeper in its own container and water gently. Sterile soil should be used to fill the pots for the individual seedlings.

When the herb seedlings are large enough and the danger of frost has passed, they can be transplanted to the garden. They should be hardened-off prior to planting outdoors. This process gradually acclimates the plant to a new environment. To harden-off, set plants outside in the shade for a few hours. Gradually increase the time outdoors as well as exposure to the sun, and in five to seven days the herb plants will be ready for the garden.

When your seedlings are large enough (as shown here), and the danger of frost has passed, they can be transplanted out in your garden.

If the weather is 70° or less, the new plants do not need to be shaded. If the weather is warm, provide some shade for a few days. In a brief period, the seedlings will adjust to their new home and manage beautifully. Refer to the herb chart (pages 183–186) for the mature size of the herbs, and space accordingly.

Cuttings

Propagation by cuttings, slips, or sprigs (they're one and the same) is an inexpensive way to reproduce identical offspring from a parent plant. Several varieties of herbs can be rooted in a glass or jar filled with water. Most of the mints can be rooted in this manner. Take a 5-inch cutting, stripping off the leaves on the bottom 2 inches. Place this in the container of water and set it on a window sill. During the rooting period, water may have to be added to the container because of evaporation. In three to four weeks there will be a large enough root mass to pot the mint in its own container. The new plant needs to be indoors for a few weeks to develop a good root system. Harden-off before transplanting outdoors.

Propagating of a cutting in its own container, or of several cuttings in a larger container, is done in the same manner. A 3-inch container is adequate for a single cutting. A plastic food container, or the plastic shoe box mentioned earlier, works very well for several cuttings. Good rooting mediums are half sharp sand, perlite, or vermiculite and half peat moss. They can be kept uniformly moist and provide good drainage and aeration. I'll discuss a single cutting, but the procedure is the same for several cuttings in a larger container.

Green, soft cuttings are the best to root. Woody cuttings are difficult: the leaves can rot before the stem forms roots. Strip the leaves off the bottom third of a 3- to 6-inch cutting. Moisten the stem and dust with a rooting powder. There are several brands of rooting powder. These powders contain root-producing hormones and are available for green softwoods and hardwoods. If you are in doubt as to the procedure, follow the manufacturer's directions. With your finger, poke a hole in a container filled with moist rooting medium and gently insert the stem. Firm the rooting medium around the stem and set the container in a small, clear plastic bag. The bag that a loaf of bread is packed in works fine. Secure the top with a wire twist, rubber band, or string and put the little greenhouse on a window sill. This little greenhouse does not need direct sun or any watering. It will stay moist for several weeks. In three to four weeks the plant will develop a strong enough root system and can be potted in its own container. The new roots should be at least ½ inch long. After a few weeks, harden-off the new plant and it can be planted in the garden.

Rooting a Cutting

Strip leaves off bottom one-third of a 3 to 6" cutting.

Dip cutting in rooting powder.

Poke a hole in the rooting medium with your finger and gently insert the stem.

Set the container in a small plastic bag and seal with a twist-tie (moisten the inside of the bag slightly).

You can put your house plants in these bags and leave for a week or two without worrying about watering.

When you leave on vacation and have a problem watering house plants, try the plastic bag method. Water your plants, let the excess drain off, and put each plant in its own plastic bag. They stay moist for several weeks.

A Propagating Greenhouse

Bench

I have a propagating misting system that is great for a small grower or hobbyist who wants to propagate cuttings all year long. My waist-high propagating bench is 2 feet wide, 8 feet long, with sides 5 inches high. The bench holds approximately 300 cuttings. The wooden bottom of the bench provides good drainage and aeration. The bench needs bottom heat in cool weather, which I provide via a watertight heating cable stapled to the bottom of the bench. The cable operates on 110 volts with a built-in waterproof thermostat preset at 70°.

It's not necessary to close in the bench. I have to because most of the time my greenhouse is open, and the wind can play havoc with my cuttings. The bench is protected with plastic. Along the length is a large piece of plastic stapled to the top. I roll up the plastic, fastening it to the top and out of the way when I'm either putting in or taking out cuttings.

Misting

My propagating greenhouse is built on the west side of the garage. I have cut a door from the back of the garage into the greenhouse. The bench has an 8-foot length of ½-inch PVC pipe with four equally spaced misters. The brass misters screw into plastic saddles that are glued to the PVC pipe. A plastic cap is glued to the far end of the PVC pipe, and a ½-inch plastic coupling is glued on the other end. From this latter connection, copper tubing is run to one end of a standard ¼" solenoid valve. The water source is on the other end of the valve.

(continued on next page)

(continued from previous page)

The time clock is wired to the solenoid valve. The time clock can be a 10-, 15-, or even 60-minute cycle. Enclosed with the clock are small metal tabs, and you can mist at the interval that suits you best. The valve has ample capacity for a much greater span than my 8 feet. A screen from the water source to the mister is a big help in eliminating fine sand grains that can plug up the brass misters. Should they plug—and I've had it happen only a few times—a needle inserted in the spray opening cleans out any obstruction.

Misting is necessary only during daylight hours. I use an inexpensive 24-hour appliance timer that starts and turns off the mister. I mist for 10 hours during the summer and 8 hours in the winter.

Rooting

I use two types of rooting powders, a number one for softwood cuttings and number three for semi-hardwood. I've had the misting system for over

Simple misting system for propagating cuttings. Bench is filled with calcined clay and holds up to 3,000 cuttings. PVC pipe suspended above the bench has brass misters inserted.

(continued from previous page)

15 years with absolutely no problems (unless someone inadvertently turns off my water source). In addition to 50 or 60 varieties of herbs, I have rooted grapevine cuttings, which take six weeks. Citrus need about eight weeks for a good root system. I've been told by an expert that you can't root citrus. This was after I had rooted and given away a few dozen orange trees. I've had fair luck with sweet bay. Year-old wood roots best, and I have had about 70 percent success. There are always two or three that root in eight weeks, but most woody cuttings take four to five months. Rooted cuttings are handled in the same manner as a single cutting in a container. In 90° plus weather, when the cuttings come out of the propagator and are potted, they go underneath the bench. It's a cool humid area, and in about five days I set them outside under the shade of my trees and shrubs.

I use a propagating medium called calcined clay that gives excellent results. I have used vermiculite and perlite, but for extended periods I've found the clay works best. It has a texture and characteristics of a medium-

Misting is controlled by a time clock, which you can set to any interval. Five seconds every 10 minutes on the time clock works fine.

(continued on next page)

(continued from previous page)

grained sand, having good porosity and permeability. It can be purchased in 50 lb. sacks at auto parts stores. They use it on driveways to soak up oil drips from cars.

Expenses

How much does all this cost? The prices below are based on 1996 costs. Most hardware stores carry PVC pipe and fittings. Brass misters and saddles can be purchased through some of the seed companies. If you have any problems, contact me and I'll put you in touch with a source.

When I decided I wanted a misting system, I didn't have several hundred dollars to invest; I had a friend design the first mister to my specifications. It's one of the best investments I've ever made.

I've noted where some of these items can be purchased. Everything else is available at hardware stores.

If you want a better bottom heat system but at a greater cost, here's an alternate. In place of the heating cable, a 22 × 60 inch rubber mat heating system is available for $97.00. You need a thermostat costing $35.00. If you do this you don't need the $16.00 heating cable, so additional cost would be $116.00. This is the system I now use. There is uniform bottom heat with the mat, and with the thermostat you have a wider range of heat. These two items are available at Park Seed.

Item	Price
Time Clock (Grainger)	$ 70.00
Timer (24 hours)	8.00
Solenoid Valve (Grainger Stock #4A692)	25.00
Heating cable 48 feet (Park Seed)	16.00
8'—½" PVC pipe	1.50
½" Plastic cap	.75
3' Copper tubing—⅜"	2.50
4—Plastic saddles @ 50¢ each (Park Seed)	2.00
4—Brass misters @ $1.25 each (Park Seed)	5.00
Connector—¼" pipe to water source	2.00
Connector—¼" pipe to ⅜" tubing	2.00
Connector—⅜" tubing to spray header	2.00
3—¼" pipes	2.00
Glue (PVC pipe)	2.00
Propagating medium	10.00
Total	$150.00 ±

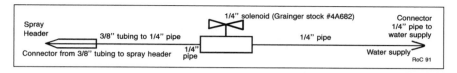

Misting system. This system is a modification of mine. It does not have as many connectors as you can see in the photograph. The solenoid is ¼" NPT on inlet and outlet with a 3⁄32" orifice similar to ASCO #83417. (ASCO makes most of the valves.) A 3⁄32" orifice will be adequate for twice the header demands of this system.

Cuttings root readily in calcined clay with regular misting.

A very simple inexpensive table-top greenhouse can be built to root 30 to 50 cuttings. Several years ago I built one to handle a number of cuttings. It works very well in temperatures ranging from 65 to 80°. The box, made of ½-inch thick redwood or cedar, is 4 inches high and 12 × 18 inches. The box should not be watertight. Drill holes in the top, two at each end of the box to accommodate bent coat hanger wire as shown in the sketch. Several cuttings are handled in the same manner as a single cutting, i.e., strip the leaves from the bottom third of the slip, moisten, and dust with rooting powder. Insert the cuttings so that there is some space between the leaves of each cutting. When the box is filled with cuttings, date and label the different varieties and place it on a large piece of plastic. Wrap the plastic around the box

Pineapple sage is one herb that roots readily in a simple glass of water.

A simple, inexpensive propagator: ½" cedar or redwood frame, approximately 4" high by 12" wide by 18" long. Drill small holes and insert wire arches (coathangers will do). Insert dusted cuttings, mist, and wrap in plastic.

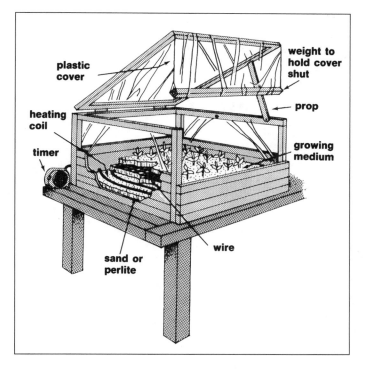

Mini electric hotbed for growing starter plants from seed.

and tie both ends. This is a larger greenhouse than the shoe-box type, but it functions in the same manner. Remember to harden-off the cuttings before putting them outside. As with seedlings, a single container or this little box shouldn't be in direct sun, but in an open area that has good indirect light. I've had excellent results using this box-type greenhouse on a picnic table on the patio beneath the overhang of our home.

Propagation in Full Sun

In the heat of summer in 90° plus temperature, you can root several varieties of herbs in full sun. A 3-inch pot with soilless mix, sand, perlite or vermiculite works fine. Wet the medium thoroughly, poke a hole in the center, and insert your rootone-dusted cutting in the hole. Firm up the soil around the cutting. Spray in the morning and evening. Your cuttings may look like the devil, but in a few weeks they will root. I have had good luck with rosemary, thyme, lemon thyme, and Mexican marigold mint. Because the cutting is rooted in this hostile, hot environment, if you use a commercial mix, you can plant directly in this ground. Water for a few days and your plants should do very well.

Scented Geraniums

Seeds are available for some of the scenteds, but propagation of cuttings is easy. The mother plant should not be fertilized ten days prior to taking cuttings. Fertilizing changes the nitrogen-carbohydrate ratio and retards formation of new roots. Cut several slips up to 6 inches long and remove the leaves on the bottom third of the stem. Don't plant for at least 30 minutes; this allows the ends to seal and improves the rooting process: cuttings develop roots in a shorter period of time, and a higher percentage will root. Insert the cutting in the medium and firm the soil or medium around the stem.

Scented cuttings can be rooted in any of the media. I use a moist soilless mix, but a container of soil with a sand center works very well. The latter method is a container of soil with a hole in the middle filled with moist sand. When the cutting has rooted in either of these, it's not necessary to transplant to another container.

Rooting powders are not necessary. They seem to hinder rather than help root formation with geraniums. I suggest rooting each cutting in its own container. You don't need to put pots inside a plastic sack, but leaves should be misted every few days, and soil should not be allowed to dry out. The cutting should root in two to three weeks. Gently tug at the slip. Resistance means the roots are forming. It usually takes four to six weeks from initial rooting time for an adequate root system to develop. Some of the leaves may yellow during this time, but as long as there are some green leaves the cutting is healthy. Scenteds need to be hardened-off prior to outdoor planting. I'm able to root scenteds from a temperature range of 60 to 85°. My greenhouse gets pretty warm, but scenteds continue to root.

When taking a cutting, I strip off approximately a third of the leaves. Because of their short, stocky stems, some of the scented geraniums may not fit that requirement: Peppermint, for example, may only have a ½- to 1-inch stem and four to five leaves. I have found peppermint-scented geraniums one of the easiest to root, but the way I propagate the coconut-scented geraniums is easiest of all. I have four hanging baskets under an overhang of my house. Coconut geranium is a trailing variety, and it flowers and drops seeds below to a prepared soil bed. When the plants have three or

Trailing coconut-scented geraniums (above) flower and drop seeds. (Below) Volunteer seedlings sprout in prepared soil bed beneath hanging baskets.

four leaves, I dig them up and plant in their own containers. I average 300 plants a year from the four baskets. They hang on a north exposure, and the small plants in the ground are hardy to at least 20°.

Layering

Layering is a method of rooting shoots while they are still attached to the mother plant. Unlike a cutting, which you detach from the parent plant and root, here the shoot is not detached until it has developed a good set of roots. Most hybrid plants do not reproduce true from seed, and layering is a good method for producing an herb identical to its parent.

Simple layering involves bending a lower branch and covering a portion of it with a light soil mix. It's a good idea to improve the soil in the area of layering. You can make a knife cut on a portion of the branch that is to be buried and dust with the appropriate rooting powder to speed up the rooting process. Most herbs will root in six to ten weeks. This varies with the type of herb, its age, and conditions during the rooting period. I rooted rosemary in a container this way and it took about six weeks.

One branch can be rooted several times, each buried portion being handled in the same manner. It may be necessary to hold or peg down the branch you're going to try to root. The branch can be held down with a fork made of wood or with wooden stakes on either side of the branch and a small piece of wire or wood over the branch secured to the top of the stakes.

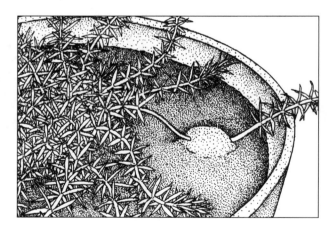

Simple ground layering of prostrate rosemary. Strip leaves off a 3 to 4″ section and cover with soil. The section will root in 6 or 7 weeks. Tug gently; resistance means roots have developed. Before transplanting, brush away soil to see if enough roots have grown, then cut from mother plant.

Sprig of rosemary with roots grown by ground layering.

Air layering is used to reproduce an offspring from a plant when this cannot be done with simple layering because the branches of the shrub or tree are too high to bend to the ground. There are not many herbs that require air layering: sassafras, sweet bay, lemon tree, and a few others may. I'll describe the technique, for it can be used to reproduce any shrub or tree.

Air layers are made in the spring on wood of the previous season's growth, or in the late summer on partially hardened shoots. The first step is to girdle or cut the bark about 12 inches from the tip end. Then remove a strip of bark an inch wide from around the stem. The exposed surface should be scraped clean to retard healing. Another procedure is to make a slanting cut a few inches long along the length of the shoot. The two surfaces are kept apart with a pebble or piece of wood. Rooting powder is dusted on the exposed surfaces. Sphagnum moss, slightly moistened, is placed around the exposed cut surfaces. If the moss is too wet, decay of the wood tissue can occur. A piece of plastic is wrapped around the shoot so that the sphagnum moss is completely covered. The ends must be sealed around the branch so that water cannot seep inside. Waterproof tape works well for wrapping the ends. Start above the plastic to be sure the ends are tight.

Root formation can be observed through the transparent plastic. Two or three months may be required for adequate root development to support the new plant, and top pruning may be necessary to balance leaf and root system. When the offspring is severed from the parent, pot it in its own container. After several weeks of hardening-off, the plant can be set out in the garden.

Air Layering

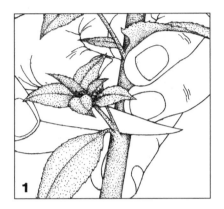

Strip off leaves at axil.

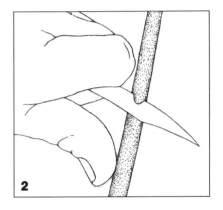

Make a sloped cut to expose cambium, insert a small pebble or stick to keep the wound open, and dust wound with rooting powder.

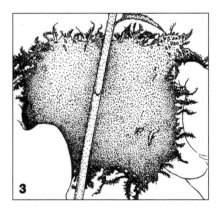

Wrap slightly moist sphagnum moss around exposed surface.

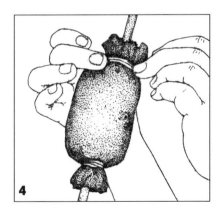

Seal sphagnum moss in plastic.

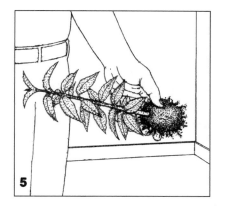 

Adequate roots will develop in 8 to 12 weeks. Sever the shoot from the mother plant and pot in its own container.

Growing Herbs in Containers

The great thing about herbs is that most of them can be grown indoors. The potting mixture discussed on page 14 is the same for any containerized herb, whether it's grown on the windowsill, patio, or under lights. A window with south exposure is best, but east or west exposures are fine, too.

Plants grown indoors should be grown in at least 6-inch clay pots. Smaller-size pots dry out faster, and your herb needs more root system than a 3- or 4-inch pot can accommodate. If you don't purchase pots but use older ones instead, scrub them clean then soak in a 10 percent chlorox and water solution. An hour or so in the solution, a few hours of drying in the sun, and the pot is ready for use. Any containerized plant needs good drainage. A few inches of gravel or small pieces of clay pots in the bottom of the container will do the job.

Factors important to growing herbs indoors include adequate moisture, periodic fertilizing, well-drained soil, and at least four hours of sun. Most plants die from overwatering. I'm asked constantly, How often should I water? When the plants need it. That's not as flippant as it sounds. There's a compulsion that every day, each and every plant has to be soaked throughly. Some days even twice. Wrong! Prior to watering, poke your finger an inch or so down into the soil. If you feel the slightest bit of moisture, it doesn't need watering. A good investment is a moisture meter. There are several brands on the market. Prices range from $10 to $20. It will pay for itself in a short time. The moisture tester usually has a metal probe 6 to 10 inches long. The probe is inserted in the soil, and the meter at the top of the probe gives a reading advising whether you need to water. Use the moisture tester for a few months and you'll develop a sense for knowing the moisture content without the tester.

There are several approaches to watering. I prefer to water from the top one time and the next time from the bottom up by setting the pot in a

You can grow culinary herbs right in the kitchen for convenience. Place some potted herbs in a box and situate near a window. Rotate the plants to promote balanced growth.

saucer filled with water. If you always water from the top, you wash the nutrients out of the soil. Continual bottom watering brings the salts to the soil surface. That's not healthy for your plants.

Indoor plants should be fertilized on a monthly basis. Fish emulsion is a good all-purpose fertilizer. Set a date: the 15th, the first of the month, whatever suits you. As long as you do it on a regular basis. Manure is another good fertilizer for your plants. A sack of composted cow manure makes a lot of tea. A cup of manure in a cloth sack, steeped in a gallon of water for an hour, makes an excellent fertilizer for any growing plant. There is no odor from composted cow manure.

Herbs grown on window sills will reach 8 to 10 inches in height. As your herbs grow, turn them every day so that the entire plant gets the benefit of the sun. If you don't turn the plant, it will get leggy and spindly. When the plant is four to five inches tall, pinch off the top. Side shoots will develop, and pinching back of some of these will make the plant bushy.

A plastic or brass mister is always helpful. Misting the leaves not only keeps them clean, but makes for a healthier plant. A small amount of mild detergent in a quart of water used as a spray on your herbs will help reduce insect problems. Don't wait till you see leaf damage to spray. Remember, no poison sprays. You will be using these herbs to flavor your food. Organic sprays are listed on pages 55–57.

Refer to the general herb chart (pages 183–186) for herbs that can be grown indoors. Some familiar ones are parsley, rosemary, thyme, chives, marjoram, oregano, sage, basil, savory, and the scented geraniums.

Artificial Lighting

Gardening under lights is the best method for growing herbs indoors. Wide-spectrum fluorescent tubes are available in many lengths, ranging from 12 to 96 inches. Indoor light gardens can be put under cabinets in the kitchen, in bookcases, on tables, in the cellar, the attic, or the garage. You can purchase free-standing, multi-tiered metal stands, equipped with casters to provide mobility. Single-fixture units for table tops are also available.

If you're handy, you can build a two-tube fixture for under $25.00, half the retail cost. The effective growing space for a dual-tube 36-inch fixture is 3 square feet. This will accommodate a dozen herbs in 6-inch pots. You'll need to hook up a timer which will turn the lights on and off at specified times to control the length of day. The timer is plugged into a wall socket, and the electrical plug of the light fixture is inserted in the timer. I use about 14 hours to grow my seedlings to about 6 inches tall and then decrease to 12 hours. When your plants are small, the lights should be a few inches away from the tops of the plants. When the lights are that close to the plants, the heat of the lamps will raise the temperature about 8°. The light fixtures should be suspended by chains so they can be adjusted to fit the height of your herbs. A general rule of thumb: set the lights the same distance from the plant as that plant's height. If the plant is 3 inches tall, the tube should be 3 inches above the top of the plant; for a 6-inch plant, the tube should be 6 inches above the top of the plant, and so on. Herbs grown under lights are cared for in the same manner as window sill plants except that it isn't necessary to rotate the containers.

Containerized Herbs (Indoors and Out)

I'm writing this chapter in our backyard, enjoying the variety of herbs we have in containers and hanging baskets: one-, three-, and five-gallon containers of sweet bay, chives, catnip, lemon balm, lemon verbena, lemon

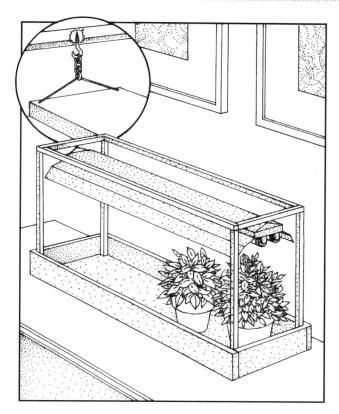

You can make this little gro-light stand for less than $15. The 24" fixture is housed in a frame of ½" thick lumber, 26" long, 18" tall, and 12" wide. Suspend the light fixture on chains slipped over screw hooks set into the top of the frame (this allows you to vary the height of the lighting). A 24" fixture on sale retails for $10–$12.

grass, lavender, rosemary, sage, thyme, several of the mints, and scented geraniums. Baskets of prostrate rosemary, mint, mixed culinary herbs, and scented geraniums hang under the overhang of our home and from the limbs of the trees. What herbs do well outdoors in containers? All of them!

Containers from 1 gallon to 40 gallon are useable. If perennials are planted in large containers, be sure they are winter hardy. If 5-gallon containers are used for tender perennials, keep them close to the front or back door. When a freeze is anticipated, they are easier to bring indoors. (Somehow, my largest containers invariably wind up the greatest distance from my garage or back door.) A planter of redwood or cedar makes an excellent container for several herbs. The planter can be divided and several herbs with similar cultural requirements can be planted together. Strawberry pots are perfect for many of the herbs. Plant the upright herbs on top and those that trail in the pockets. For hanging baskets, the upright herbs go in the middle (parsley, chives, or garlic chives), and trailing or semi-trailing vari-

Be creative with your containers—the characteristics of the herbs are diverse, and your containers should be, too. On shelf (left to right): oregano, tarragon, nasturtium. Clockwise from front: mint, lemon grass, prostrate rosemary, basil, anise, parsley, bay, lemon verbena, lavender. Sage, thyme, marjoram, and chives grow in crock; dittany of Crete spills out of hanging basket.

eties go around the edge (mints, prostrate rosemary, oregano, marjoram, catnip, lemon balm, savory, or whatever suits you). A large shallow clay pot is attractive and useful for several of the herbs.

Regardless of what type of container you use, there are a few basic requirements. Good drainage—whether the container is clay, plastic, or an unusual material—is a must. A few inches of gravel or broken bits of clay pots at the bottom of the container will provide good drainage. You'll want your herbs to get four or five hours of sun. They'll grow in full sun, but will dry out very quickly in the hot summer. Daily care is required. By daily care I mean checking your containers every day. Herbs in gallon size containers need to be watered every day in the summer; 3- and 5-gallon containers require water every second or third day. All containerized herbs need to be fertilized on a regular monthly basis.

If you want to make some hanging baskets, here are a few tips. Soak adequate sphagnum moss in a large bucket of water for 15 minutes. Squeeze

A redwood planter box is an attractive way to containerize compatible herbs. This box, 4' long, 1½' wide, and 2' high, contains chives, thyme, parsley, and tarragon.

Large strawberry pots are ideal for miscellaneous herbs. Plant upright herbs on top and those that trail in the pockets.

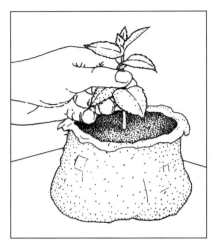

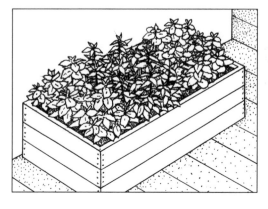

To plant mints in a container
with other herbs, set the plant
in a plastic bag filled with soil
and then plant the bag;
otherwise, the mints will make
short work of their neighbors.

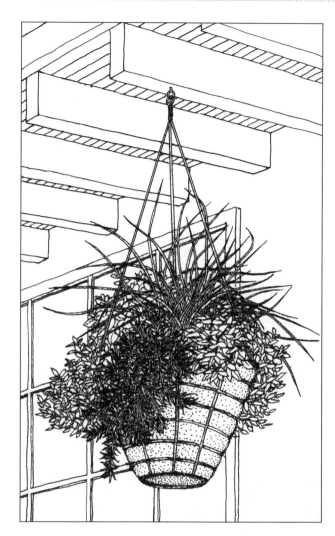

Herbs will grow in hanging baskets, too. Line the baskets with 2–3" of moist sphagnum moss, fill the remainder with soil, and plant. Prostrate rosemary, oregano, mints, thyme, geraniums, dittany, and chives are all good candidates.

out the excess water and layer the moss in the wire basket. There should be at least a 2- to 3-inch thickness of moss. Add the proper amount of soil, and plant the herbs.

My first few baskets were frustrating. I had trouble fastening the wire to the outside rim of the basket so it would hang straight. I'd fasten one wire, but then the other two required adjusting and readjusting. After half a dozen baskets, it came to me. It's very easy. Hold the end with the closed loop in

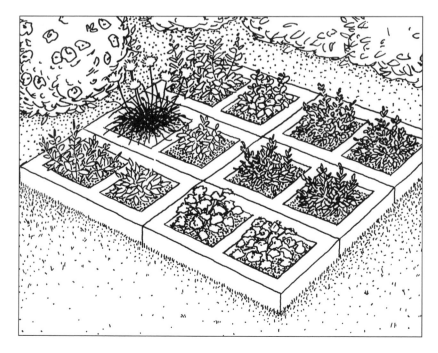

Cinderblocks make interesting dividers for outdoor herb plantings. They can be set above ground to line a walk or patio or to border a raised bed; buried in the ground, they make attractive designs and facilitate culture of herbs with different requirements. They are especially good for planting mints in with other herbs because the roots of mint will strangle out other herbs in the garden.

one hand and, get this, bend all three wires at the other end at the same time. A three- or four-inch bend is adequate to fasten the wires securely.

Be creative with your containers. I have seen commodes, chests of drawers, iron kettles, old watering cans, and many other unusual pots. As long as the container has a hole or holes in the bottom and is at least 6 inches deep, it can grow herbs. A sectioned cinder block setting on the patio, or buried in the ground, makes a fine container for several of the mints. The root system of mints can take over the garden. Mints can be planted in a plastic bag of soil and then set in a large container with other herbs. The bag will restrict the root system but should be open so the mint can be watered.

Harvesting, Drying & Storing

Most of the herbs can be used fresh to flavor your food. In Zones 6, 7, and 8, you may want to dry some for use during the winter. The herbs are simple to harvest, dry, and store. Herbs should be harvested just prior to flowering, when they contain the maximum amount of essential oil on which fragrance and flavor depend. The mints, however, have their richest oil content when they flower. In Texas, most herbs yield several crops a growing season.

You can prune approximately a third of the plant without interfering with continual production. Stop pruning early enough to allow growth prior to the first frost. If you prune right up to frost time, plants can suffer winterkill. In Zones 9 and 10, winters are mild enough to allow pruning of most of the perennials for almost 12 months of the year. Harvest a quantity that you can manage for that day. If you gather too much, the leaves can rot. Mid morning is a good time to harvest the leaves. Prune a third of the plant, and if it's not quite dry or if the leaves were dirty and you hosed them off, hang in the open shade to dry.

I'll discuss several methods of drying; choose the method that suits you. The drying process requires good ventilation, heat, and absence of dust. I've hung stalks and leaves in my garage, but it's too dusty and I had to discard what I tried to dry. Label what you're drying, dried leaves all look alike and some fragrances are similar. You don't want to flavor a roasting chicken with catnip instead of basil.

The quickest way to dry herbs is in the oven. The clean leaves should be stripped from the stalks, put on a cookie sheet or pan and set in the oven. The door should be open an inch or so, with temperature set at 100°. A single layer of leaves will dry in about 90 minutes. If you have several layers of leaves stacked in one pan, it takes forever to dry. A word of caution on oven drying. The fragrance of some of the herbs will permeate the entire

51

The simplest and quickest way to dry herbs is in the oven. Set the temperature at 100° and leave the oven door open slightly. Allow 45–90 minutes, depending on the amount of leaves.

house. When I dry basil in the oven I do it when my wife is out for a few hours. The strong odor really bothers her.

During the hot summer, herb leaves can be dried in the back of your car. Spread newspapers on the back seat and the floor and place a single layer of leaves on the newspaper. Keep the car closed up when you're not driving, and in three or four days the leaves will dry.

An attic is a good area to dry stalks of leaves; if it has cross ventilation, is free of dust, and over 90°, leaves can be dried in a week. Hanging herbs outdoors is not a particularly efficient way. If it rains and you don't protect them in time, you have to start over. I have dried stalks and leaves in a large paper sack. The stalks and leaves are placed in the sack, with the top of the stalks near the bottom of the bag. The bundle is tied with string at the opening of the bag. This is labeled and hung in a warm area. It takes several weeks to dry herb leaves in such a manner. Regardless of what method of drying you use, the herbs should be dried as quickly as possible, in very little sun, so that the volatile oils and original green color are retained.

A friend who lived in Italy for a number of years told me how Italians dried basil. Leaves are placed in large crocks, alternating a layer of leaves and a layer of salt. When the basil leaves are to be used, the salt is shaken off the required amount of leaves needed.

When the herb leaves are dry, shred them between your hands or through a coarse sieve. Whole leaves, for tea, can be stored without shredding. The stems of the herbs contain essential oils, too, and you can put leaves and stalks through a vegetable chopper. This method applies to small-leaf herbs such as savory, thyme, marjoram, and compact bush basil.

Store your dried herbs in clean, opaque, tightly capped bottles. If clear bottles are used, store them in the pantry or cupboard. Examine the bottle of dried leaves in a few days. If there is any moisture on the inside of the bottle, they need additional drying. Low heat in the oven, with the door open a few inches, should completely dry the herbs in 30 to 60 minutes. Let them cool, place them in the bottle, and check for moisture in a few days.

Seeds collected for storage are harvested and dried in a manner similar to the method used for leaves. The seed heads should be cut when the seeds

This dried basil has just been chopped and is ready for storing in a small apothecary jar.

first turn brown. If you wait too long, the wind will get most of the seeds. I cut the entire seed head and drop it into a large paper sack. I label the bag and hang it in my garage. They're dry in about six weeks. Screen the seeds through a large sieve. Save some in a metal or plastic container for next year, and enjoy the rest. Caraway, dill, fennel, anise, and cumin are some of the seeds you can collect. If you dry seeds in the oven, they can't be used in the garden next spring.

Dig up the roots of plants such as comfrey and horseradish and wash thoroughly, removing all dirt. Large roots can be split or sliced and placed on a screen. The screens can be placed outdoors in the shade and brought indoors in the evening. The root sections need to be turned every few days, and in three or four weeks should be partially dry. Place the roots in the oven, at low heat, with the door open a few inches to complete the drying. Roots should be stored in airtight containers. (Large mason jars make excellent storage jars.) Don't store leaves, seeds, or roots in paper envelopes or cardboard boxes. If dampness doesn't cause mold, the bugs will chew through these containers and help themselves to your delicious dried herbs.

Many of the herbs can be frozen. Some of these are chives, garlic chives, dill, basil, and tarragon. Cut the stems with adequate foliage, washing the dust and soil from the leaves. Tie some string around several stems and dip in boiling water for about 60 seconds. Remove and either cool the herbs under the tap or dip in a pan of cold water for a minute or two. Pick off the leaves and place them either in foil or freezer bags, labeling each bag for storage in the freezer.

Using Your Herbs

Herbs That Help Your Garden Grow

Herbs can be quite beneficial in your garden. Not only can herbal sprays and powders be used to combat insects, but certain plantings of herbs along with vegetables can actually help the vegetables to grow.

Herbs as Insecticides

In most of Texas we have longer growing seasons, which means larger harmful insects and more of them. Some of the herbs are effective organic insecticidal sprays and do not leave a harmful residue. Here's how to prepare a good garlic spray: Take 5 ounces of chopped garlic cloves and let them soak in 4 teaspoons of mineral oil for 24 hours. Then slowly add 1 quart of water in which ½ ounce of oil-base soap (Palmolive is good) has been dissolved and stir well. Strain the liquid through fine gauze, and store in a china or glass container (garlic reacts with metals). Try it against your worst pests, starting with a dilution of 1 part insecticide to 25 parts of water. Continue diluting until you reach the proper proportions to control the insects. I would estimate that approximately one part garlic concentrate diluted with 50 parts of water is a good mix.

Cayenne (hot pepper) is effective against several of the garden pests, namely ants, caterpillars, cabbage worms, and tomato worms. Mix 1 cup each of peppers and water, straining the mix through gauze to eliminate the solids. Add ½ teaspoon of soap powder or mild detergent and the spray is ready to use. Dry cayenne dust can be used as a deterrent for insects on several of the garden vegetables. Shred and dry the pods of cayenne. Low heat in the oven for a brief period will hasten the drying process. The dust will adhere better to the foliage if it is wet. You will need to re-dust after a rain. Wash your hands thoroughly, several times, after handling hot peppers. If you don't, and inadvertently rub your eye, it can be very painful.

Herbal teas are fairly effective against garden pests. Steep equal amounts of herb leaves and water for 24 hours. Strain the mixture through gauze or cheesecloth. Chive tea is used to control leaf and fruit scab, horseradish against fungi, hyssop against bacterial diseases, and wormwood tea is used to control aphids and caterpillars that attack the leaves of fruit trees.

Essential oils of many herbs are known to have insecticidal properties. A 2 percent emulsion spray of the oil of lemon grass was found to be highly effective on red spider and aphids. Sprays of mint, coriander, sage, and savory had moderate success against these pests. Oil sprays of a number of herbs work on mosquitoes. Elecampane is the most effective, but oils of basil, sage, marjoram, and rosemary will work, too. Insects have been repelled with oils of pennyroyal, thyme, lavender, bay, sassafras, and other herbs. Leaves of mint, lavender, sage, and wormwood can be used in the closet to protect woolens from the moths. Sprinkle liberal quantities of leaves among the clothing. This smells better than mothballs, and you'll probably attract members of the opposite sex when you wear these fragrant garments.

I don't use any poison sprays in my garden, but when I see the first signs of insect damage I use an organic powder called rotenone. It is effective for all sucking insects that attack vegetables. This powder, marketed by several manufacturers, is derived from the roots of several species of trees in the genus *Lonchocarpus,* including cube from Peru and timbó of Brazil. This insecticide can be used to control aphids, spider mites, chinch bugs, cabbage worms, mosquitoes, and even flies. Rotenone, used in normal concentrations, is not considered harmful and can be used up to 24 hours before harvest.

Another herb that is a very effective dust for destructive insects is pyrethrum, a perennial chrysanthemum (for details on the plant, see page 155). It is a short-term dust, breaking down quickly in sunlight. It is used to control cabbage worms, leaf hoppers, spider mites, and aphids as well as many household pests. Nicotine can be used against white flies, thrips, spider mites, and aphids. I have read that Mexican marigold (*Tagetes minuta*) is highly effective and very similar to pyrethrum. In parts of Africa it is used to repel flies, fleas, and lice by hanging dried leaves in the problem areas. I located a seed source and am growing, experimenting, and tabulating the results with this herb. Don't confuse this with Mexican marigold mint (*Tagetes lucidia*), a lovely perennial. The latter has yellow button-like flowers and foliage with a licorice fragrance.

I have mentioned several herbal sprays and organic powders to help control destructive insects. I say *control,* for total elimination is unnecessary. One reason we don't need total elimination is that natural pruning is beneficial for many of the vegetables. We've been brainwashed to think that if

Herbs That Get the Bugs Out

Pest	Helpful Herb	Remarks
Ants	Pennyroyal, mints, tansy	Plant near entries and around perimeter of house.
Aphids	Garlic, nasturtiums	Garlic should be planted close to rose bushes so that the garlic leaves touch the bushes. Plant both herbs near broccoli. Random plant garlic throughout garden.
Carrot fly	Onion family (onions, chives, garlic chives, shallots, leeks), rosemary, sage, wormwood	In and about the carrot patch.
Cucumber beetle	Radishes	Not an herb, but deters this pest. Scatter seeds in cucumber patch. Eat some radishes, but leave some to help cucumbers.
Flies	Tansy	Plants should be near entries to the house.
Flea beetle	Wormwood, mint	Interplant with lettuce.
Fleas (on your pet)	Pennyroyal	Rub leaves thoroughly on coat of your pet.
Japanese Beetle	White geranium	Plant near plants bothered by this pest.
Mosquitoes	Sassafras	Rub leaves on exposed skin.
Nematodes	French marigold	Plant around main stalk of tomato plants.
Squash bugs	Nasturtiums	Plant several around the main roots of the squash plants.
Weevils	Garlic	Scatter cloves in problem food area.
White cabbage Butterfly	Sage, rosemary, hyssop, thyme, mint, wormwood	Interplant to protect members of cabbage family (broccoli), cauliflower, Brussels sprouts).

there's a blemish on a fruit, it's no good, or that a head of lettuce is unfit to eat if there's a hole or two in a leaf. It just isn't so.

Companion Planting

Several of the herbs are great companion plants for certain vegetables. Some herbs hinder the growth of some vegetables. Combinations of certain varieties of herbs are beneficial; other groupings are not. Alphabetically listed below are some helpful plantings and some to avoid.

Anise—does well with coriander
Basil—don't plant near rue
Chives—helps the growth of carrots
Coriander—retards growth of beans and tomatoes
Caraway—does not do well near fennel
Dill—aids cabbage, but suppresses carrots
Fennel—bad influence on beans and tomatoes
Garlic, chives, leeks, and shallots—inhibit beans and peas
Hyssop—increases grape crop, decreases carrot crop
Mint, rosemary, and sage—aid cabbage family
Parsley—helps tomatoes
Rosemary and sage—help each other
Southernwood—plant near cabbage
Wormwood—plant off in a corner
Yarrow—increases fragrance of most herbs

Several of the herbs act as trap crops, i.e., the harmful insects are attracted to them instead of nearby vegetables. Mustard and nasturtium attract several of the destructive garden insects. They are particularly useful planted near cabbage, cauliflower, Brussels sprouts, broccoli, and radish. African marigold and white geranium attract and kill the Japanese beetle, and lemon grass repels the African tsetse fly.

Some, but not enough, experimenting with herbs as natural insecticides is being done. Hopefully, this research will expand and more ways to use herbs and other plants as natural repellents will be discovered.

Herbs That Refresh and Soothe

Many herbs can be used to soothe the body and the spirit. They are nature's own comforter.

Herb Oils

Commercial herb oils are extracted by distillation. If you don't own or have access to a still, here's a method that will enable you to extract the oil of many herbs. Use a gallon-size ceramic crock, filling it with clean leaves and blossoms of the herb of your choice. Use rain or distilled water, pouring enough in the crock to cover the material. The crock should be set outdoors in the full sun. Should it rain, either cover your crock or bring it indoors. In five to eight days a scum, the herb oil, will form on the surface of the water. You can soak up the oil with a cotton ball and carefully squeeze the liquid into a small container. Inspect your crock on a daily basis, removing the oil as it forms with the cotton and transferring it to the smaller container. Over an extended period you may have to add more rainwater to the crock. When the oil appears to be extracted from the crock, usually after several days, place gauze or cheesecloth over the mouth of the small container of herb oil. This will allow the water that is mixed with the oil to evaporate. In about a week you should have pure herbal oil that can be transferred to a small, clean opaque bottle with a tight-fitting lid. It is now ready for use or storage.

Herbs that lend themselves to extraction of oil include mints, thyme, basil, marjoram, sage, lemon verbena, lemon balm, and many more. Oils from fragrant woods can be extracted in the above manner, too. The wood needs to be reduced to shavings prior to filling up the crock.

Herbal Baths, Rinses, and Body Lotions

Camomile, lemon verbena, and rosemary make excellent rinses for the hair. Blondes can use rinse of camomile flowers to bring out the highlights. Rinses are easy to make with herb leaves and tender tips. Use either rain,

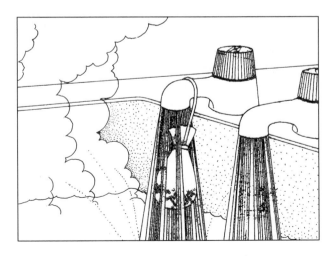

Place a gauze bag filled with dried leaves of your favorite herbs and hang it over the spout of your tub. You'll smell nice all over.

distilled, or softened water (there are too many harsh chemicals in most tap water). Simmer 2 cups of the leaves in a quart of water for 30 to 60 minutes. When your mixture is cool, strain off the liquid and store in a clean container. It's available when you are. I've mentioned a few herbs, but there are many more that make fragrant hair rinses.

Body lotions (pomades) are not difficult to prepare. Leaves of the mints, marjoram, lemon balm, lemon verbena, lavender, pineapple sage, scented geraniums—the list is endless—all make lovely fragrant body lotions. Blend two cups of your favorite herb or herbs with a small amount of alcohol. Plain alcohol can be purchased at any drug store. Add enough alcohol to your mix to fill up an inch or so of a quart bottle. Cap this bottle tightly and shake it vigorously every few days over a couple of weeks. At the end of two weeks, strain off the liquid into appropriate bottles.

Does an herb bath appeal to you? You can boil a gauze bag filled with 2 to 3 cups of a fragrant herb for 20 minutes, pouring the liquid in the full tub of water. Another method is to take the same gauze bag with herbs and hang it over the spout, allowing the warm water to pour through it. Not only will you smell nice, but an herb bath is most refreshing. You can use some of the same herbs that are used for body lotions.

Aromatherapy

My friend, Lucia Bettler, owner of Lucia's Garden and a certified aromatherapist, passed on this information to me. Aromatherapy is the art of using pure plant essential oils because these oils reflect the essence of the plant. The oils are extracted by either steam distillation or cold expression (or see my method on pages 58–59).

According to Lucia, different oils can create different feelings. They can change an emotion, calm, cheer, comfort, enhance, inspire, refresh, rejuvenate, rouse, stimulate, strengthen, or uplift a mood.

You know with all the information Lucia gave me about aromatherapy, not one herb oil could knock off 40 years from my age and make me 38 again. Such is life.

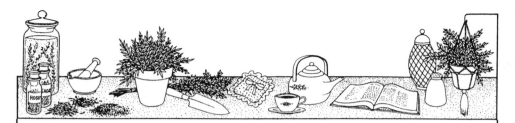

Potpourri

A potpourri is simply a collection of dried fragrant leaves and stems that one keeps in pretty jars. When you want to turn on your olfactory senses, take off the top and breathe the exotic fragrance. They are easy to make, and here are a few basics. Early in the morning, pick the leaves and petals of your fragrant herbs and/or flowers, discarding the brown blossoms. Collect a lot more than you think you'll need because there's quite a loss in volume when they dry.

Place the leaves, stems, and petals on a clean paper or cloth in a warm place and out of bright sunlight. Stir the mix a few times a day to allow all material access to air so it can dry. Just as you dried herbs for storage, you can hang small bunches of stems with leaves and flowers in a warm, clean airy garage or attic. Some people like to dry orange or lemon peel for their potpourri. Make sure you scrape and clean off all the pulp.

(continued on next page)

(continued from previous page)

Potpourri needs a fixative added to retard evaporation of the essential oils. Orris root and gum benzoin are used for this purpose and can be purchased at drug stores or health food stores. Use ½ ounce of fixative for each quart of potpourri. I would suggest you use gum benzoin, for orris root can irritate the skin.

When your herbs are completely dry, mix them with the fixative in a large wooden bowl. When you mix or store herbs, never use a metal container. Wood, ceramic, plastic, glass or enamel are fine. Put your ingredients in a large container with a tight cap and store in a cool place. Every four or five days, take a wooden spoon and stir the contents. If you see any moisture, place the herbs on papers again to dry (if your mix isn't completely dry, it will mold). In six to eight weeks you can put the potpourri in smaller attractive containers.

Teas

There are two methods in making tea: *infusion,* where boiling water is poured over the leaves until it is strong enough, and *decoction,* where the water and herb are boiled to bring out the oils. The best container for preparing tea is either porcelain or glass—never metal. Fresh or dried leaves and flowers can be used. Mix your own special brand of herb tea. Keep a record of the different combinations you try and eventually you'll find your favorites. Half a dozen herbs will make a large number of combinations, all different in taste.

Teas used for relief of colds include catnip, yarrow, lemon balm, and sage. Lemon balm, peppermint, rosemary, lemon verbena, and marjoram are teas that have a calming effect. For years, wintergreen tea has been used for relief of rheumatism. My favorite herbal tea is lemon grass; the leaves can be dried in a week or so in the open shade in hot summer. Spread the leaves out on a newspaper and move it inside if it looks like rain.

Herbal Dyes

Many of the herbs produce such fine colors that they are used for coloring and dyeing. A fixative, or mordant, is necessary in the process, for not

Plant	Part Used	Color
Agrimony	Entire herb	Yellow
Daphne	Seed	Yellow
Date palm	Roots	Brown
Elecampane	Roots	Blue
Eucalyptus cineria	Leaves	Red, yellow, gold
Hops	Stalks	Brownish-red
Hyssop	Leaves plus copperas	Green
Indigo	Plant	Blue
Juniper sp.	Berries	Yellow or brown
Lily of valley	Leaves	Green
Marigold	Flowers	Yellow
Parsley	Leaves	Green
Rhododenron	Leaves	Gray
Safflower	Flowers	Yellow
Saffron	Flowers	Yellow
Tansy	Stalks plus alum	Green-gray
Yarrow	Flowers plus alum	Yellow
Yarrow	Leaves	Green
Yellow flag	Roots plus sulphate of iron	Black
Zinnia	Flowers	Yellow

only will it fix the color but in many instances it will bring out a brighter and sharper color. I suggest that if you are interested in pursuing this further, get a book on dyeing. Listed above are some herbs, flowers, vegetables, and trees that are used for dyes, stains, and inks.

Reputed Herbal Medicinal Properties

"Reputed" is a common word used in describing medicinal properties of many of the herbs. There are some really vague expressions regarding herbal curative properties. But many of the herbs *do* have excellent medicinal properties, and I'll list some at the end of this discussion. Here are some other phrases commonly used.

This herb is *known medicinally,* or this is an *ancient known stimulating tonic plant.* Back in Roman days, *Pliny told us elecampane would relieve indigestion.* (I'm skeptical of today's attorneys; why should I listen to one from 1900 years ago?) Another herb is said *to relieve indigestion.* Who said so?

The juice of this particular herb is said *to be a good medicine for diarrhea,* and the juice of another is listed as *an aid for diarrhea.* A certain nut is mentioned, and if they are eaten in quantity, *laxative effects may be noted.*

The mints are *seemingly all good for aiding digestion*. Seemingly? What does that mean? And yet another: Everyone knows *it stimulates the appetite*. An herb is mentioned as an aid to rheumatism, but a footnote tells us one reference says it's not too reputable. Here's one for our part of the country: In the South where the magnolia grows, reports are that *the mild astringent qualities of the leaves are an alleviant for rheumatism*. The juice of another herb is *thought to be good for rheumatism*.

The best one is out of an herbal remedy book in my library. At the end of the book is a bibliography with works from Moses up to modern authors. Some of the references include the Scriptures, Culpeper, and Gerard. The author *dares the reader to challenge the validity of the authorities cited*. A couple of his works have "author unknown." I can't challenge them.

In my opinion, there are too many medicinal qualities attributed to the herbs, and, unfortunately, these appear to many people as factual. But many herbs *do* have medicinal value, and a large number are being researched. I've mentioned that aloe vera is good for burns. Garlic juice was used as an antiseptic during World War I. The oil of certain species of the eucalyptus is used as an astringent. Jewel weed (impatiens) is good to treat poison ivy. The juice from the stems dries up this painful skin irritation. If you have been in the woods and think you were exposed to poison ivy, oak, or sumac, it's a good idea to use the juice on exposed portions of your body.

I suggest that you check the reported medicinal qualities of many herbs before relying on them to benefit your particular ailment. Enjoy growing them, smelling them, tasting the culinary ones. Be careful when you use any medicine, herbal or otherwise.

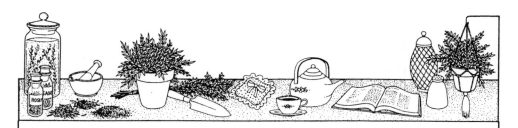

Herbal R_x

Historically, the most important uses of herbs were medicinal. They have been prescribed to treat human infirmities for at least 5,000 years. The sixteenth century was the great age of herbals, and it's these texts that hold, in my opinion, the most interesting and unusual potions to aid or cure ailments ranging from ingrown toenails to noises in the ears.

Among many uses of sweet marjoram, Culpeper tells us:

It is warming and comforting in cold diseases of the head, stomach, sinews, and other parts taken inwardly or outwardly applied. The decoction thereof being drunk, helps diseases of the chest, obstructions of the liver and spleen, old griefs of the womb, and the windiness thereof, and the loss of speech, by resolution of the tongue. Made into powder, and mixed with honey, it takes away the marks of blows and bruises. It is good for the inflammation and watering of the eyes, if mixed with fine flour and laid into them. The powder snuffed up into the nose provokes sneezing, and thereby purges the brain.

I like what Culpeper says about southernwood:

The ashes mixed with old salad oil (not new or fresh, but old), *helps those that are bald, causing the hair to grow again on the head and beard.*

Did you see my picture? Didn't work on my head. I guess it only half works. Here's what he has to say about tobacco:

The smoke of tobacco injected in the manner of a clyster, is of efficacy in stoppage of the bowels, for destroying small worms and for the recovery of persons apparently drowned.

A priceless prescription, author unknown, for constipation:

(continued on next page)

(continued from previous page)

Take an equal amount, preparing as a tea, of each of the following—wormwood, wood betony, bugle, mountain mint, germander, hyssop, ground ivy, yarrow, periwinkle, marjoram, rosemary, sanicle, sage, thyme, vervain, catsfoot flowers, and coltsfoot flowers.

To be honest, I'm afraid to try this.

There are some unusual potions for treating premature wrinkles, wounds, warts, to purify the blood, expel worms, to restore normal functions of the body, and on and on. An herbal text written in the early 1600s compiled an index of diseases and herbs that can cure them. I've listed several that, in my opinion, are fascinating.

Disease	Herb(s) That Cure	Comments
Baldness	Beets, yarrow	Doesn't work
Belchings	Betony, burnet	Burnet is great in salads
Blastings by lightning	Purslane	No comment
Bad breath	Mint, rosemary	They both work
Forgetfulness	Agrimony	I forgot if it works
Baldness	White mustard	No way
Lust	Hemlock	It's a poison; it'll stop you forever
Sun-burnings	Betony, cucumber	This could be the answer

A Word of Warning

The yew (*Taxus baccata*) is included here as a warning—it is deadly poisonous. This applies to all parts of the tree, even those that appear in ancient herbals as cures for one thing or another. Its delicate pink seeds and dark green leaves have tempted many children with tragic consequences.

I point out yew, but many of the old herbal texts list all sorts of potions for several plants that are poisonous. Many folks enjoy collecting wild herbs these days, but a number of plants in the field and forest can be fatal. All parts of the buttercup, if ingested, can severely damage the digestive system. Jimson weed—the entire plant—has proven to be fatal in many instances. From time to time I read in the newspapers that someone has become very ill or has died from collecting and eating wild mushrooms. *Be very careful* of old herbal remedies, and *absolutely* identify any wild plant that you intend to either eat or use in a tonic or potion.

An herb that can cause skin problems is *Dictamnus Albus,* whose names include fraxinella, burning bush, and dittany. It is a showy herbaceous perennial with fragrant ash-like leaves and many large flowers. The flowers of the *rubra* variety are pink; those of *alba* are white. This plant can cause painful burns and leave residual skin discoloration for months. Three prerequisites for skin disorders caused by this herb are moist skin from water or sweat, contact with the plant, and exposure to the sun. I suggest that if you grow this herb, wear gloves, a long sleeve shirt, and don't perspire when pruning or even getting near it.

Cooking with Herbs

Many of the recipes in this section are from restaurants in Houston. All of them are from innovative chefs who skillfully use herbs to import delectable flavors and aromas to their dishes. The Vallone restaurant group includes Tony's, Anthony's, La Griglia and Grottos. The Carrabbas restaurants are in Houston as well as many cities in Texas. They are also in Colorado, Florida and Georgia. Joey's of Dallas has been kind enough to add to this collection. My wife and I have eaten at all of these restaurants over the years and they are all four star. We have not eaten at Joey's in Dallas. But, hey! He's a Vallone so you know you can expect great food.

John Greene, my nephew in New York, an artist and sculptor, has taken his talent to the kitchen as well and is a premier chef. In addition to his recipes, h' has included a paragraph on using dried herbs that is very enlightening.

My wife, also a wonderful cook, has supplied one of her recipes.

Boulevard Bistro
Houston

Herbed Crab Cakes

1	cup shrimp or lobster shells
1	cup cream
1	jalapeño
1	ounce lemon grass
1	red pepper, brunoise
1	yellow pepper, brunoise
1	bunch green onion, minced (green only)
1	tablespoon lemon juice
1	pound lump crabmeat
1	egg
½	cup toasted bread crumbs
	Cayenne, salt, pepper
	Chopped herbs (cilantro, parsley, chives, dill, marjoram)

Combine shrimp or lobster shells with cream, jalapeño, and lemon grass. Reduce by half. Strain and chill.

Sauté peppers and green onion in 1 tablespoon of olive oil. Chill.

Combine all ingredients and form into 2-ounce cakes. Bread lightly in cornmeal flour. Pan fry in clarified butter.

Mint Julep

1	ounce whiskey (bourbon, a blend, or scotch)
6	mint leaves (spearmint is best; others are suitable)
1	teaspoon sugar

Make a syrup of half the liquor, mint leaves, sugar and a small amount of water. Add the syrup to a glass half filled with crushed ice. After stirring, add the balance of the whiskey and more crushed ice. Stir final mix, or use a shaker, and it's ready for consumption. You may want to increase or decrease the number of mint leaves to suit your taste.

Cafe Annie
Houston

Mussel Soup with Cilantro and Serrano Chile   *Serves: 6*

Cilantro Puree

4	large bunches of cilantro, roughly chopped
½	bunch parsley, roughly chopped
¼	yellow onion, roughly chopped
2	cloves of garlic, roughly chopped
2	serrano chilies (stems removed)
½	cup fish stock

Place all of the ingredients in a blender and puree with just enough fish stock to form a very thick and smooth puree.

Ancho Chile Jam

1	pound ancho pepper
2	tablespoons vinegar
¼	cup honey
1	shallot
1	clove garlic
3	ounces red currant jelly

Soak ancho peppers in warm water until very soft. Drain off the water and puree the chilies in a blender with the vinegar, honey, shallot, garlic and jelly. Continue to puree until very smooth and thick. Adjust honey or vinegar to balance spiciness and tart/sweetness.

To Prepare the Soup

60	mussels, cleaned
1	cup fish stock
	Cilantro Serrano Puree
3	cups cream

Place the mussels in a small soup pot with the fish stock. Cover and bring to a boil. Steam the mussels until the shells are just opened. Remove the mussels from the pan and remove the mussels from their shells. Boil the liquid in the pot to reduce it to approximately 1 cup. Add the cream to the stock and boil until the liquid is very slightly thickened. Add enough Cilantro Puree to the pot to thicken the soup. Bring the liquid to a boil for a few seconds. Place the warm mussels in the bottom of the six soup bowls. Pour the hot soup over the mussels. Fill one mussel shell with Ancho Chile Jam and lay the shell on top of the mussels so that it does not sink into the soup. Garnish with cilantro leaves and serve.

Cafe Annie
Houston

Red Chile Soup with Cilantro Cream

Makes approximately 1 gallon

6	ancho chilies (3–4 ounces total), stemmed and seeded
2	pasilla chilies (2 ounces total), stemmed and seeded
2	chipotle chilies (¼ ounce total), stemmed and seeded or substitute small can of chipotle)
2	sweet red peppers (10–12 ounces total)
2	tomatoes (1 pound total)
1	red onion (8 ounces), peeled
2	cloves garlic, peeled and quartered
1	large sweet potato (10–15 ounces), peeled and cut in large cubes
2	stalks celery, roughly chopped (6 ounces)
1	carrot, peeled and coarsely chopped (5–7 ounces)
1	bunch cilantro, chopped (4 ounces)
	Chicken stock (4–6 cups)
2	cups cream
2–3	tablespoons pure maple syrup
	Lime juice (1–2 tablespoons)
	Salt and pepper to taste

Note: Other dried red chilies may be substituted for some of the chilies (except ancho) if they are not available.

Lightly toast the chilies in a warm skillet. Roast the red peppers over an open flame to char the skins. Place the red peppers in a bowl and cover with a kitchen towel. Allow the pepper to steam under the cloth to loosen the skin. Peel and seed the peppers. Broil the tomatoes, onion, and garlic until the tomato skins are blistered and the onion and garlic has softened. Combine the broiled vegetables with the other vegetables in a soup pot and cover with chicken stock. Bring the stock to a boil and simmer until all of the vegetables are cooked (about 30 minutes). Strain the soup and puree the solid ingredients in a food processor until very smooth. Add the puree back to the liquid and chill. Stir in the cream, maple syrup, and lime juice. Salt and pepper to taste. The amount of maple syrup and/or lime juice may be altered to adjust the spiciness. Chill the soup and serve cold with the Cilantro Cream.

Cilantro Cream

2	bunches cilantro (with some leaves for garnish) (8 ounces)
½	bunch parsley (2 ounces)
1	serrano chile (or substitute jalapeño) (½ ounce)
¼	cup chicken stock
1	cup sour cream or creme fraiche

Garnishes

1	Ancho Chile
	Cilantro sprigs

In a blender, puree the cilantro, parsley, and chile in the chicken stock. Add extra chicken stock if necessary to get the ingredients to puree in the blender. Slowly whip this puree into the sour cream. Salt and pepper to taste. The consistency of the cream may be adjusted with additional stock or sour cream. The cream should be of similar consistency to the soup. Float the cream on top of the soup creating an interesting design. Garnish with a very thin julienne of ancho chile and some cilantro leaves.

Riviera Grill
Houston

Poached Garlic-Tomato Vinaigrette

½	cup garlic cloves
1½	cups chardonnay wine
2	bay leaves
¼	cup virgin olive oil
¼	cup chardonnay vinegar
1	teaspoon aged balsamic vinegar
1	teaspoon chopped fresh thyme
1	teaspoon chopped fresh basil
1	teaspoon chopped fresh marjoram
1	teaspoon sugar
	Salt and pepper to taste
⅓	cup peeled, seeded, finely chopped tomatoes

Peel the garlic and thinly slice across the grain. In a non-reactive pan combine garlic, wine, and bay leaf. Poach the garlic for 3–5 minutes or until tender. Remove garlic with a slotted spoon and reserve. Boil the wine until reduced to 2 tablespoons. Remove the pan from the heat and whisk in the oil and vinegar. Stir in the reserved garlic.

Note: This vinaigrette tastes best if made one day ahead.

Cafe Annie
Houston

Warm Semolina Cakes with Three Cheeses   *Serves: 6*

The Cakes

2	cups milk
½	teaspoon kosher salt
	Pinch white pepper
	Pinch freshly grated nutmeg
½	cup semolina
6	tablespoons unsalted butter
1	cup freshly grated Parmesan cheese
2	egg yolks
6	ounces chevre (goat cheese) in a log shape

The Peppers

1	sweet red pepper, seeded and diced
1	sweet green pepper, seeded and diced
¼	cup fresh basil, chopped
4	green onions, chopped
½	cup virgin olive oil
6	ounces mozzarella cheese, grated

The Cakes

In a deep saucepan, combine the milk, salt, pepper, and nutmeg. Bring to a boil and slowly add the semolina while stirring constantly. Stir over moderate heat until the semolina becomes very thick and "pulls" away from the sides of the pan. Remove from heat and stir in butter. Add 2 tablespoons of the Parmesan cheese, and mix in egg yolks one at a time. Turn into a bowl, cover and refrigerate until cooled and set. By hand, shape into a dozen balls and pat into 2½-inch cakes.

In a large skillet sauté semolina cakes in 2 tablespoons of butter over moderate heat for about two minutes on each side or until golden brown. Remove to a baking pan and place a slice of goat cheese on top of each cake. Bake in a 350° oven until goat cheese is warm.

The Peppers

In a skillet, sauté peppers, basil, and green onions in olive oil until warm and the aroma of the peppers and basil is evident.

To serve, place two semolina cakes on each plate and sprinkle with mozzarella cheese. Spoon the warm olive oil and pepper mixture over the top of each cake. Sprinkle with remaining Parmesan cheese.

Poblano Chile Salad with Dried Fruits

6	chicken thighs
2	large red onions, sliced
6	poblano chilies
3	red bell peppers
1	jalapeño chile
12	dried figs, cut into small pieces
12	dried apricots, cut into small pieces
¼	cup raisins
¼	cup roasted pecans, coarsely chopped
1	bunch cilantro, coarsely chopped
¼	cup walnut oil or more if desired
1	lime
	Salt and pepper
1	head red lettuce, washed
2	bunches watercress, thick stalks removed
1	cup sour cream

Over a charcoal fire,* grill the chicken thighs and slices of red onion until done. Allow to cool. Oil the chilies and red bell pepper and grill over the hottest part of the charcoal fire until the skins are lightly charred and blistered. Place the peppers in a bowl and cover with a kitchen towel and allow to cool. When cool, peel the poblano chiles and red bell peppers.

Filling for the poblano chile

Finely mince the jalapeño chile. (Caution: after grilling, this chile will be very spicy). Cut the chicken meat from the thigh bone and coarsely chop the meat. Coarsely chop half of the grilled red onion. In a bowl, combine the chicken meat, dried fruits, chopped red onion, pecans, chopped cilantro, and minced jalapeño chile. The amount of jalapeño chile added can vary with the degree of spiciness desired. Add 2 tablespoons of walnut oil and the juice of ½ lime and mix thoroughly. Salt and pepper to taste.

Make an incision in the chilies and remove the seeds. Fill the chilies with the meat and fruit mixture.

Finishing the Salad

Remove the core, stem, and seed from the red bell pepper. Cut the meat into thin strips. Combine the red leaf lettuce, watercress, the remaining red onion, and the red pepper in a bowl. Add two tablespoons of walnut oil and the juice of ½ lime. Add a pinch of salt and some ground pepper and toss to combine.

Presentation

Place the tossed lettuces on one half of a large plate and stuffed chile on the other half. Garnish with sour cream and sprigs of cilantro.

---

*These items may also be cooked in a broiler. The procedure is essentially the same.

Cafe Annie
Houston

Grilled Quail with Black Bean Torta and Poblano Sauce

Serves: 6

The Quail

12	quails, boned
2	ancho chilies (1 ounce)
1	cup peanut oil (or ½ peanut oil and ½ olive oil)
1	clove garlic
½	orange (¼ cup juice)
1	lime

Black Bean Tortas
Refried Black Beans

4	ounces black beans (½ cup)
1	clove garlic
1	sprig epazote
1	ounce bacon, diced
1	ounce lard, diced
1	tablespoon butter
3	eggs, beaten

Guacamole

2	avocados, 8 ounces each
½	red bell pepper (4 ounces), finely chopped (½ cup)
1	small red onion (6 ounces), finely chopped (1 cup)
2	serrano chilies (substitute jalapeño), minced
1	bunch cilantro, chopped (4 ounces or approximately ¾ cup)
1	lime (2 tablespoons)
2	tablespoons olive oil
1	teaspoon salt and pepper to taste
3	ounces goat cheese
½	cup sour cream
12	flour tortillas

Sauce

3	poblano chilies, 3 ounces each (6 ounces peeled, seeded, and chopped)
1	red onion, sliced (6 ounces)
4	tomatillos, husks removed (10 ounces)
2	cloves garlic (½ ounce)
½	cup pumpkin seeds (2 ounces)
1	tablespoon maple syrup (to balance acidity and spiciness)
1½	cups chicken stock
2	bunches cilantro, chopped (1 to 1½ cups) reserve some sprigs for garnish
4	tablespoons unsalted butter
1	tablespoon kosher salt

Tomato Salsa

6	plum tomatoes, chopped (1 pound or 2 cups)
½	red onion, minced (½ cup)
1	bunch cilantro, chopped (¾ cup)
1	serrano chile (substitute jalapeño), minced (2 teaspoons)
1	lime (2 tablespoons)
	Salt and pepper to taste

The Quail

Wash the ancho chilies and remove the stems and seeds. Soak the chilies in water for 5 minutes to soften them. In a blender, puree the ancho chilies, garlic, orange juice, and the juice of the lime with the oil. Marinate the quail in the puree for about an hour.

The Black Bean Tortas
Refried Black Beans

Place the black beans, garlic, and epazote in a pot with 2 cups of water. Bring to a boil and simmer until the beans are soft. If necessary, add just enough additional water to keep the beans covered. When the beans are done, allow them to cool in their own liquid. When the beans are cool, puree half of them in their liquid until smooth. Combine the puree with the whole beans.

In a heavy skillet or pot, combine the bacon and pork fat and cook over medium heat to render the fat. Add the cooked beans and stir the mixture over medium heat until the fat is absorbed and the mixture is thick. If the beans are too liquid, continue to cook slowly over medium heat to evaporate the liquid until the mixture is thick.

In a clean skillet, heat the butter until hot. Add the bean mixture and heat until hot. Add the beaten eggs and scramble with the beans. Add the salt and transfer to a plate and keep warm.

Guacamole

Split and seed the avocados. Remove the meat to a mixing bowl. Add the sweet pepper, red onion, serrano chile, cilantro, and juice from the lime to the avocado. With back of a large spoon, mash the ingredients into a very coarse puree. Salt and pepper to taste.

To Assemble the Tortas

With a 2-inch cookie cutter or small knife, punch out 12 small rounds from the tortillas. Spread some black beans (approximately 2 tablespoons) on one tortilla. Add a nugget (½ ounce) of goat cheese to the black beans and top with the avocado mixture. Finish the tortas by covering the avocado mixture with a second small tortilla. In a large flat skillet, heat a tablespoon of butter over moderate heat. Slowly fry the tortas on both sides until the tortillas are golden brown. Keep warm.

The Sauce

Grill the poblano chilies over a charcoal fire or under a broiler until the skins are charred. When cool, peel and seed the chilies. Grill or broil the onion slices, tomatillos, and garlic cloves until lightly cooked. Heat the pumpkin seeds in a dry skillet until lightly toasted. In a blender, combine the chilies, tomatillos, onion, garlic, maple, and one half of the pumpkin seeds with the chicken stock. Blend briefly (10 seconds) to give a coarse puree. Do not over blend. Transfer the puree to a sauce pot. If the puree is too thick, add more stock; if it is too thin, boil gently to reduce to a sauce-like consistency. Just before serving, heat the sauce over moderate heat. Add the chopped cilantro and the remaining pumpkin seeds and whip in the butter. Salt and pepper to taste.

Tomato Salsa

Roughly chop the tomatoes. Combine with the minced onion, chopped cilantro, and minced chile. Add the juice of the lime and mix thoroughly. Salt and pepper to taste.

To Assemble the Dish

Grill the quail, skin down, over a charcoal fire or skin up in a broiler on a wire rack. The quail should be cooked almost entirely on the skin side. Grill the quail on the meat side for only a few seconds. This will prevent the meat from becoming too dry. The meat should be pink and not over-cooked. Depending on the temperature of the fire, three to four minutes should be sufficient.

Place a warm black bean torta in the center of each dinner plate. Top each torta with some sour cream. Spoon some sauce onto each plate around the torta. Place a grilled quail on each side of the torta. Garnish with the tomato salsa and some sprigs of cilantro.

Cafe Noche
Houston

Tortilla Soup

4	tablespoons epazote, chopped
12	ounces dried pinto beans
2½	white onions, quartered
8	whole garlic cloves
3	tomatoes, roasted
1	ancho chile
4	tablespoons olive oil
1¼	quarts chicken broth
	Salt to taste

Cook beans in three quarts of water with the epazote, onion, 4 cloves garlic, and salt to taste for 1½ hours, until tender. Remove from heat and let cool. Put beans in blender.

Blend onion, 4 garlic cloves, tomatoes, and chile in blender.

Heat oil in large saucepan and pour in tomato mixture. Cook over low heat for 10–15 minutes. Add bean puree and simmer until thick. Add chicken broth and salt to taste. Stir and heat for 10 minutes.

Garnish: shredded chicken, corn, lime wedges, Monterey Jack cheese, cilantro, chips.

Carrabbas
Houston

Pollo Arrosto   *Serves: 10*

1½	ounces fresh rosemary leaves
1½	ounces fresh Italian parsley leaves
1½	ounces fresh basil leaves
20	cloves garlic
½	cup grill seasoning
½	cup lemon pepper
10	half chickens
	Grill baste
	Lemons

On a cutting board, finely chop the rosemary, parsley, basil, and garlic together.

Mix grill seasoning and lemon pepper together.

Working with one half chicken at a time, sprinkle one heaping tablespoon of the grill seasoning/lemon pepper mixture under skin and over entire chicken half.

Use one tablespoon of chopped herbs and garlic mixture again under skin and over entire chicken.

Brush lightly with grill baste and squeeze the juice of ¼ of a lemon over chicken. Repeat for the rest of the half chickens.

Bake in a preheated 400° oven for 50–60 minutes. Store covered in a warming drawer.

Herb Butters

You can make a zesty spread of your favorite herbs. Simply boil some dry leaves in a little water, drain, and blend briskly with butter. Use enough butter to suit your taste; three ounces of butter to two ounces of herbs makes a pleasing, yet not overseasoned, spread. This recipe is also excellent if you substitute cream cheese for butter.

To make a herbal fondue, follow the same procedure with the herbs, and add to your favorite cheese melted in a double boiler. Add wine, beer, or milk to give the fondue the consistency and taste you like.

Carrabbas
Houston

Baste for Grill

Yields approximately 3 cups

1	pint extra virgin olive oil
10	cloves peeled sliced garlic
3	whole hot red peppers
3	tablespoons fresh rosemary
1	teaspoon dried oregano
10	whole black pepper corns, crushed
5	bay leaves
	juice of 2 lemons

Over a low flame, sauté garlic slowly until garlic begins to color. Remove pan from heat and add remaining ingredients.

Carrabbas
Houston

Grill Seasoning

Yields approximately 1¾ pounds

1	pound kosher salt
8	ounces black pepper
3	ounces granulated garlic
1	ounce dry oregano

Place all ingredients in a mixing bowl. Mix well.

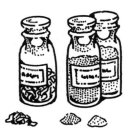

John D. Greene
New York

Fusilli with Olive Puree, Red Onion, Tomatoes, Basil, and Bacon/Pancetta
Serves: 4

4	slices pancetta or bacon, cut ¼ inch thick
1	medium-large onion, diced
3	tablespoons extra virgin olive oil
3	tablespoons red wine vinegar or balsamic vinegar
1½	teaspoons brown sugar
¼	teaspoon salt
1	pound fusilli (or any other pasta, preferably a short one)
1	28-ounce can crushed tomatoes, drained
6	tablespoons olive puree or olive paste
½	cup fresh basil leaves, chopped, plus 4 sprigs of basil to garnish
	Freshly ground black pepper

Bring a large pot of salted water to a boil.

While the water is boiling, cook the bacon/pancetta in a skillet until crisp, or in the microwave for 6–7 minutes. Drain and break into ¼-inch pieces.

Meanwhile, in a skillet (not aluminum) sauté the red onion in 1 tablespoon olive oil, until golden (do not brown).

In a separate pan, combine the vinegar, sugar, and salt and bring to a boil.

Add the fusilli to the large pot of boiling salted water and cook until barely tender. At the same time, add the tomatoes to the vinegar mixture and simmer until the liquid is reduced.

In a small bowl, blend together the remaining olive oil and olive puree/ paste. In a heated serving dish, toss drained pasta with this mixture. Add half the chopped basil, and half the tomato mixture, plus a grinding of pepper, and toss. Add the pancetta and mix with the remaining tomato mixture and chopped basil. Garnish with the fresh sprigs of basil and serve.

John D. Greene
New York

Chilled Minted Pea Soup *Serves: 4*

2	tablespoons unsalted butter
1	small onion, finely chopped
1	head of bibb lettuce (or any sad-looking leftover lettuce leaves)
3	cups of tiny fresh peas (3 pounds in the pod) or 2 packages frozen peas (10-ounce size), thawed
2	cups chicken stock or canned broth
½	teaspoon sugar
¼	teaspoon salt
⅛	teaspoon freshly ground pepper
¾	cup heavy cream
1	tablespoon freshly chopped mint, plus 4 sprigs of mint to garnish

In a large heavy saucepan, melt the butter over moderate heat. Add the onion and cook, stirring, until softened but not brown (about 8–10 minutes). Add the lettuce and cook, stirring, until wilted (about 1 minute).

Add the peas, chicken stock, sugar, salt, and 1½ cups of water. Bring to a boil over high heat, reduce the heat to moderate, cover and simmer until the peas are very tender (8–10 minutes for fresh peas, and 3–5 minutes for frozen peas).

Strain the soup. In a food processor, puree the solids with 1 cup of the cooking liquid. Pass this puree through a sieve into a large bowl. Gradually stir the rest of the liquid into the puree, mixing well.

Add the cream, mint, pepper, and additional salt to taste. Let cool to room temperature. Cover and refrigerate until well chilled (at least 6 hours, or overnight).

Stir and adjust the seasoning, if necessary, before serving. Garnish with the fresh sprigs of mint.

John D. Greene
New York

Herbs "Fried" in Olive Oil

While using my microwave to warm up a dish of extra-virgin olive oil with herbs in it—which we serve in our house with bread in lieu of butter—I made a wonderful discovery! I had not only made a delicious dish of dipping oil, but also had created "fried" herbs, which can be used separately as a garnish. Simply fill a small bowl with oil, put a few sprigs of any herb into it (I have used rosemary, sage, parsley, basil, and chervil), and cook for 20 seconds to 1 minute. Serve the oil and/or herbs immediately.

Herbed oil is also wonderful as a sauce for vegetables such as asparagus or artichokes, and can even be used on fish or chicken, perhaps with a pinch of cayenne pepper added to the oil.

If you use parsley, you can serve it as a separate side as well as a garnish

John D. Greene
New York

The Storage and Use of Dried Herbs

Most of us have a drawer full of dried herbs that are so old that the companies that bottle them are no longer in business! Dried herbs, unlike fine wine, do *not* age in the bottle (or in the plastic bag or container) and are meant to be used soon after they are purchased. I suggest you buy small amounts of dried herbs, as you need them, because after a few months they begin to lose their intensity. Further, you might try crumbling the dried herbs before you use them, and remember, when making a stew or a fricasee, to add the dried herbs toward the end of the cooking process, except for bay leaves, which get put in at the beginning but must be removed before serving. An even better idea, if you grow your own herbs, is to freeze them at the end of their growing season, and take them out and wash and use as needed (basil, however, is best frozen with water in ice cube trays).

Samuel Hudson
Houston

Black Bean and Pumpkin Soup

1	pound black beans, washed and picked over
1	teaspoon salt
3	tablespoons unsalted butter
1½	cups finely chopped onions, preferably yellow
5	large cloves of garlic, minced
1	cup raw green pumpkin seeds (Likely source: health food store, organic market)
¾	cup canned tomatoes, drained
1	cup canned pureed pumpkin (usually found with canned pie fillings)
6	ounces boiled ham, cut into ⅛-inch cubes
2½	cups beef stock (Campbell's beef broth is fine)
1	tablespoon ground cumin
2 to 4	tablespoons lemon juice
	Black pepper, preferably freshly ground
½ to1	cup medium sherry
2 to 4	tablespoons extra virgin olive oil

Follow quick-method directions on 1-pound bag of dried black beans, or place 1 pound of dried black beans in a heavy pot and cover with boiling water to a level of about 2 inches above the beans. Add 1 teaspoon of salt, return to the boil, then lower heat and simmer, partially covered, for about 2–3 hours or until the beans are tender *but not mushy*. Add more water if beans become dry.

Meanwhile, melt the butter in a heavy skillet over medium heat. When it has foamed, stir in the onions and minced garlic and sauté 8 to 10 minutes, until lightly colored.

Toast the pumpkin seeds (can be prepared ahead). Preheat oven to 400°. Pour raw green pumpkin seeds into large flat-bottomed pan, stir in 2 to 3 tablespoons of extra virgin olive oil, then smooth seeds out. Place pan on center rack of preheated oven, toast for 10 to 18 minutes, stirring occasionally. Toast seeds to a uniform shade of rich, deep brown.

When the beans are tender, stir in the tomatoes and transfer to a blender with a steel chopping blade. With a few on-off motions, process until the beans have started to smooth out but still are somewhat chunky. This will have to be done in batches. Return the beans and tomatoes to the pot and stir in the pumpkin, ham, and 2½ cups of stock.

Add the sautéed onions and garlic, ground cumin, 2 tablespoons lemon juice, salt and pepper, and mix well. Bring this mixture to a boil and then reduce heat and continue cooking uncovered for another 20 to 25 minutes, stirring occasionally, scraping sides and bottom of pot as you stir.

Stir in the sherry and taste for salt, additional lemon juice, and other seasonings. If soup is too thick, add stock or sherry. If too thin, continue to cook until thicker. Stir in toasted pumpkin seeds, heat through.

Serve it forth. Partake of it with wise and merry friends.

Tony Chachere
Cajun Country Cookbook

Fried Shrimp

1	lb. fresh shrimp
2	tablespoons vinegar
1	small can evaporated milk
2	eggs
1	tablespoon Calumet baking powder
1	cup flour
	Tony's Creole Seasoning to taste
	Season to taste

Make a mixture of eggs, evaporated milk, baking powder, and vinegar. Marinate shrimp for at least one hour. Remove and season lightly with Tony's Creole Seasoning. Dip in flour and fry at 380° for not more than 10 minutes.

Joey's
Dallas

Herb Encrusted Spa Salmon with Red Pepper Saffron Essence

6	ounces red bell peppers
10	ounces lobster stock
1	teaspoon saffron
	Cracked black pepper
2	tablespoons arrowroot and 2 ounces cold water
1	tablespoon each herbs picked from stems (chives, basil, oregano, thyme, parsley, rosemary)
4	8-ounce Atlantic salmon filets (bones and skin removed)

Dice red peppers, place in lobster stock with saffron and simmer until peppers are pliable. Puree pepper mix in blender, return sauce to stove and bring to a full boil. Thicken with arrow root and water mix. Strain through chinoix and keep warm.

Cut all herbs together until finely chopped. Crust salmon in herbs until well-coated. Sear in hot sauté pan with 1 tablespoon vegetable oil to crust the herbs. Bake in 400° oven until firm.

Serve over grilled vegetables of choice with red pepper saffron essence. Garnish with sprigs of fresh assorted herbs.

Camille Waters

Deep Squash

Steam six medium-sized whole zucchini. With a spoon, scoop and hollow zukes so they resemble boats. Put scooped zucchini innards in skillet with:

6	green onions, chopped
4	stalks celery, minced
1½	lbs. boiled srimp
4	tablespoons butter
½	cup toasted bread crumbs

Sauté. Add 1 teaspoon dill (½ teaspoon dried) or ½ teaspoon basil or ¼ teaspoon white pepper. Add 1 cup grated monterrey jack cheese. Mix. Put stuffing into boats and bake 20 minutes at 350°. Serve with gazpacho or cold plum soup.

Joey's
Dallas

Herb Roasted Chicken

1	2½-pound whole chicken
2	basil leaves
½	orange cut into sections
2	cloves of garlic

Marinade

⅓	cup lemon juice
1	cup orange juice
½	cup honey
4	tablespoons chopped garlic
¼	cup Dijon mustard
½	cup chopped oregano, basil, parsley, thyme (combined)

Place basil leaf, orange section, and garlic clove under skin of the chicken breast on each side of the bird.

Combine all ingredients in marinade together.

Marinate whole chicken in marinade for 24 hours. Drain well.

Roast in oven at 350° until golden brown and crispy (approx. 2 hours).

Serve with lemon or orange segments to squeeze over chicken.

Pancho Garrison, Chef
Houston, TX

Flounder with Sage

Lightly flour a filet of flounder and drop in pan with some butter. Add several fresh sage leaves. Keep flame at about medium force. Turn fish over after a few minutes. Salt. Remove when fish is cooked—it should be slightly crisp on the outside. Squeeze juice from half a lemon in pan and deglaze pan with a few drops of water or white wine, stirring everything stuck to the bottom of the pan into a delicious sauce. Pour over the filet of flounder.

La Mora
Houston

Pesto di Funghi e Olive

Yields: 2 cups

6	cups coarsely chopped cremini mushrooms
1	heaping tablespoon chopped garlic
1	tablespoon shallots
4	ounces olive oil
1	heaping tablespoon fresh Italian parsley
1	teaspoon chopped fresh rosemary and sage
1	tablespoon lemon juice
1	tablespoon salt
1	teaspoon pepper
1	cup pitted black olives (Calamata)
1	tablespoon lemon juice
¾	cup olive oil

In a large sauté pan, put 4 ounces olive oil, the garlic, shallots, parsley, sage, and rosemary. Bring to heat together. When the garlic starts to sizzle, add the mushrooms. Add salt and pepper. Stir constantly. When mushrooms begin to brown and soften, add the lemon juice. Cook until most of the pan juices have evaporated. Remove from heat and let cool.

Chop the pitted black olives very fine. Place in a large mixing bowl.

When the mushrooms have cooled, chop them very fine. Combine them thoroughly with the chopped olives and ¾ cup of olive oil.

This makes an excellent topping for crostini (toasted rustic bread slices) and for grilled fish, and chicken. It also can be tossed with pasta.

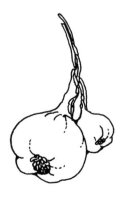

La Mora
Houston

Salsa di Pomodoro for Crostini

Yields approximately 4 cups

½ cup finely chopped garlic
4 anchovies
½ cup extra virgin olive oil
4 cups diced ripe Roma tomatoes
¼ cup coarsely chopped fresh basil
¼ cup coarsely chopped Italian parsley
1 ounce balsamic vinegar
1 ounce lemon juice
  Kosher salt and freshly ground black pepper, to taste
  Crostini

Place garlic, anchovies, and cold olive oil in a skillet over medium heat. As oil heats up, the anchovies will begin to dissolve. Mash them, incorporating them into the olive oil and sauté garlic until soft but not colored. Remove from heat and let cool.

Place diced tomato, fresh basil, parsley, balsamic vinegar, lemon juice, salt and pepper in a large bowl. Combine thoroughly.

When olive oil mixture has cooled, add to tomato mixture. Combine thoroughly. Allow to sit for a couple of hours before serving so that flavors will intensify.

Crostini

Preheat oven to 375°. Slice day-old bread about ¼ inch thick. Brush with olive oil. Place on cookie sheet in oven and toast until golden brown, about 10 minutes.

Mandola's Family Table Restaurant
Houston

Mama's Stuffed Eggplant   *Serves: 4*

1	medium eggplant
1	pound lean ground beef
1	medium onion
3	cloves garlic
3	tablespoons chopped Italian parsley
3	tablespoons chopped fresh basil
2	eggs
1	cup unseasoned bread crumbs
1	cup grated Romano cheese
2	cups homemade pomodoro sauce

Cut eggplant in half lengthwise and boil in lightly salted water for 5 minutes. Remove eggplant and let cool. Scoop pulp out of eggplant leaving about ½ inch from the skin and chop pulp.

Chop onion and garlic fine and place in the bottom of a large skillet. Place meat on top of onion and garlic and brown meat. Add eggplant pulp and salt and pepper to taste and continue cooking for another 15 minutes.

When meat and eggplant mixture is finished cooking, drain fat and let cool. Place stuffing in a mixing bowl and add parsley, basil, eggs, bread crumbs, and cheese. Mix and adjust seasoning.

Stuff eggplant halves and place eggplant in baking dish. Pour tomato sauce (pomodoro sauce) over and cover casserole. Bake for 45 minutes in a 350° oven.

Massa's Restaurant
Houston

Stuffed Quail with Crawfish Dressing *Serves: 4*

8	whole quail, raw semi-boneless
½	cup fresh rosemary
½	cup butter
1	cup celery, chopped with tops
1	cup onions, chopped
½	cup green onions, chopped
¼	cup garlic, chopped
½	cup basil, chopped
1	pound crawfish tails, peeled and precooked
1	cup cracker meal, or crushed crackers
2	eggs, raw
	salt
	black pepper
1	12-ounce can bing cherries, for sauce (optional)

Rub quail with rosemary, black pepper, and salt. Prepare stuffing by sautéing remaining vegetables and basil in butter until tender. In mixing bowl combine sautéed vegetables with cracker meal, crawfish, eggs, salt and pepper to taste. Mix well. Stuff quail liberally and bake in 350° oven for 45 minutes or until done. Don't overcook. Baste with butter once while cooking. Place cooked quail on bed of brown or wild rice. Cherry sauce is optional.

Herbal Dip

2	cartons (6 oz.) cottage cheese
1	cup diced cucumber
¼	cup chives
¼	cup parsley
1	tablespoon salad burnet
1	tablespoon borage
¼	cup chopped radishes

Chop the herbs finely, and blend all the ingredients thoroughly. Chill, and garnish with parsley, nasturtium buds, or whatever you like. You can add lemon juice, milk, or wine to liquify further. Play around with this recipe: add whatever suits you. Chopped nuts, watercress, shallots, garlic—the list of alternatives or additional ingredients is limitless.

Moose Cafe
Houston

Smoked Chicken Pomodoro   *Serves: 2*

12	roma tomatoes, fresh (blanched and peeled)
3	cloves garlic
¼	cup basil, fresh (chopped)
1	teaspoon oregano, fresh (chopped)
1	teaspoon white pepper
¼	cup onion (chopped)
1	cup olive oil
	Salt to taste

Put all ingredients except oil in food processor. Puree until moderately smooth. Then, with machine running, gradually add oil. Remove and check salt. Store chilled.

4–6	ounces pulled smoked chicken, or cubed smoked chicken breast or turkey
8	ounces cooked fettuccini or fusilli pasta
1	tablespoon olive oil
	Parmesan cheese

Heat oil and sauté chicken or turkey to heat through. Add 1 cup sauce to chicken, then pasta. Heat through. Put in warm bowl, top with Parmesan and garnish with fresh basil leaves.

Nash D'Amico
Houston

Grilled Chicken in Herbs
Chix Herb
Serves: 1

8	ounces boneless chicken breasts, grilled
2	ounces garlic, sliced
½	ounce olive oil
1	tablespoon rosemary, (mixed well with garlic)
1	pinch white pepper and seasoned salt, (in mixture)

Char chicken breast on char grill. Then take off grill, brush with olive oil mixture including spices.

Place on baking pan and finish cooking in the oven for about 5–8 minutes until golden brown. Take out of oven and drain off excess oil, place on platter and serve with side of linguini pesto.

Nash D'Amico
Houston

Garlic and Parsley Pasta Pazzo
Serves: 1

1	tablespoon butter
3	ounces fresh mushrooms, sliced
1	tablespoon chopped scallion onions
2	ounces stock
2	ounces white wine
2	ounces tomatoes, fresh diced
6	whole green olives
½	fresh lemon, juice only
2	ounces canned artichoke hearts, sliced
½	teaspoon fresh chopped basil
¼	cup pasta
1	sprig chopped parsley, for garnish
1	pinch white pepper
1	pinch seasoned salt

Heat butter in sauté pan. Add mushrooms and scallion onions to pan and sauté for about 2 minutes.

Deglaze with stock and white wine. Add tomatoes, olives, butter, lemon juice and artichoke hearts.

Reduce for one minute. Add basil. Continue reducing until sauce "creams out."

Add pasta and toss coating well.

Lift pasta out with fork and using slotted spoon remove ingredients from sauce and place on pasta.

Pour enough remaining sauce over pasta to coat.

Sprinkle with parsley for garnish.

Nash D'Amico
Clear Lake

Chicken Grandezza

Serves: 1

8   ounces chicken breasts
2   ounces butter
2   ounces white wine
1   ounce stock
3   whole plum tomatoes, with juice
4   sprigs fresh oregano
2   canned artichoke hearts packed in water, sliced
1   pinch fresh oregano, chopped
1   pinch fresh basil leaves, chopped
1   teaspoon salt and white pepper

Season chicken with salt and pepper. Rub with olive oil and grill.

For sauce, place wine, stock, tomatoes (crushed by hand), and artichoke hearts in sauté pan. Reduce by half. Add butter and oregano.

Place chicken on plate. Top with sauce.

Omni Houston Hotel
Houston

Thyme-Garlic Tomatoes Confit

Serves: 4

6	each large Roma (plum) tomatoes (peeled)
1	ounce picked fresh thyme
6	cloves garlic, finely diced
4	ounces olive oil
	Sea salt and fresh ground pepper to taste

Preheat oven to 400°.

To peel tomatoes, cut a small crosshatch slit in bottom of each tomato and immerse in boiling water for 30–40 seconds; then immerse in iced water. Peel and reserve.

In a flat sauté pan, place the Roma tomatoes (split in half), cut side down.

Sprinkle tomatoes with chopped thyme and garlic.

Season with salt and pepper.

Coat tomatoes with olive oil and place in a hot oven to roast until they begin to soften, approximately 6–8 minutes.

Remove from the oven and serve immediately.

Note: The remaining liquid from the confit process is wonderful tossed with pasta or your favorite vegetable.

Pancho Garrison, Chef
Houston, Texas

Pesto Sauce

Blend together:

4	tablespoons chopped fresh basil
1	tablespoon chopped pine nuts
3	tablespoons Parmesan
3	garlic cloves
6	tablespoons olive oil
1	tablespoon chopped parsley
1	tablespoon Pecorino cheese (a goat cheese)

Cook pasta—preferably homemade fettuccini. Mix with sauce, butter, plus some of the boiling water you cooked the pasta in. Serves three or four.

Omni Houston Hotel
Houston

Basil-Infused Oil

>Fresh basil
>Extra-virgin olive oil

Blanch herbs (with stem) in boiling water for 30 seconds. Remove from water with a skimmer and quickly refresh them in an ice bath to stop cooking. Drain them well of all liquid.

Measure the herb mixture, place in blender, and add an equal amount of fruity extra-virgin olive oil. Puree to a smooth, well-ground mixture. Remove from blender and add four times as much olive oil as the amount of paste. Blend well and store for one day.

Without stirring up sediment, skim off all infused oil and strain through a coffee filter. Store oil in refrigerator for up to two weeks.

Omni Houston Hotel
Houston

La Reserve Thai Pesto

6	cloves garlic
2	jalapeños (de-seeded)
	Zest from one lemon
2	cups packed basil
½	cup packed cilantro
½	cup roasted pine nuts
¼	cup coconut flakes
¼	cup packed mint
2	tablespoons minced ginger
4	ounces lemon juice
	Kosher salt to taste
¾	cup extra virgin olive oil

Put through meat grinder (smallest grate plate), then combine in a food processor and slowly add olive oil and lemon juice to taste.

Tony Mandola's Gulf Coast Kitchen
Houston

Chicken Cacciatore   *Serves: 6*

3	ounces olive oil
1	whole chicken
12	each pearl onions
2	each green and red bell pepper, sliced long
½	tablespoon salt
½	tablespoon black pepper
2	ounces fresh garlic, sliced
¼	cup fresh basil
1	cup red wine
8	green olives with pimento
½	cup black olives
30	ounces pomodoro sauce
10	ounces mushrooms, cut in half
¼	cup parsley

Flour for chicken

½	pound flour
2	tablespoons salt
2	tablespoons black pepper
2	tablespoons granulated garlic

Remove legs and wings from chicken. Cut breast and thighs into eight pieces. (Total yield from chicken will be 12 pieces.)

Roll chicken pieces in seasoned flour.

Heat a 16-inch skillet and add 3 ounces of seasoned olive oil. Brown the chicken pieces on high heat. The dark meat (thighs, drumstick) takes a little longer, so start with the drumsticks for 5 minutes. Add the thighs and cook 5 minutes. Add all the white meat. Pull all pieces except drumsticks at 17 minutes. Cook drumsticks 5 more minutes. Turn the pieces in the skillet so they do not burn. Total cooking time will be 22 minutes.

Remove chicken pieces when they are done. Leave the drippings in the skillet. Add pearl onions and sauté with the chicken drippings until they are soft (4 minutes), caramelizing them.

Add bell peppers, all salt, pepper, sliced garlic, and ⅛ of the basil. Simmer and mix (2–3 minutes).

Deglaze the pan with ½ of the wine. Add olives, basil, suga, mushrooms, parsley and bring to a medium heat. Simmer 30 minutes.

Place on serving dish and top with parsley.

Vallone Restaurant Group
Houston

Pasta Al Limone
(Lemon Pasta)

Serves: 4–6

1½	cups heavy cream
6	good-sized lemons
½	cup unsalted butter
4	tablespoons freshly squeezed lemon juice
1	cup freshly grated Parmesan cheese
	Crushed red pepper flakes
	Thin lemon slices for garnish
1	pound linguine, fedelini, and spaghettini

Put the cream in a small saucepan and simmer for 10 minutes over medium heat or until thickened. Rinse the lemon thoroughly and wipe dry. Grate the lemons and put their zests into another small saucepan. Add the butter and melt over very low heat. Do not brown. Set aside both saucepans.

Return the just cooked "al dente" pasta to its pot over low heat immediately after draining and toss with the lemon juice and cheese. Add the butter and zest and toss, then add the cream. Sprinkle with crushed red pepper flakes and garnish with lemon slices.

Vallone Restaurant Group
Houston

Grilled Sea Bass with Anchovy-Balsamic Dressing

Serves: 4

½	cup olive oil
2	large garlic cloves, minced
5	canned anchovy filets, drained, chopped
¼	cup balsamic vinegar
2	tablespoons chopped fresh oregano or
2	teaspoons dried oregano
4	6-ounce sea bass filets

Heat oil in small skillet over medium-high heat. Add garlic and sauté for 1 minute. Add anchovies and whisk until anchovies dissolve, about 2 minutes. Cool 1 minute. Whisk in vinegar and oregano. Season with salt and pepper.

Prepare barbecue (medium-high heat) or preheat broiler. Brush sea bass with 2 tablespoons dressing. Season with salt and pepper. Grill or broil fish until cooked through, about 4 minutes per side. Pass remaining dressing separately.

Rio Ranch Restaurant
Houston

Rio Ranch Cowboy Beans

1   cup dry kidney beans or pinto beans
6   cups water
2   ancho chiles, stemmed, seeded, and chopped
2   ounces bacon, diced
1   bay leaf
1   sprig epazote, chopped (optional)
1   tablespoon salt
2   tablespoons brown sugar
1   white onion, chopped
8   Roma tomatoes, chopped
6   cloves garlic, chopped
2   chipotle chiles (canned), chopped (optional)
1   tablespoon dried oregano
½   teaspoon comino seeds, toasted
2   teaspoons salt
1   teaspoon black pepper

Combine all the ingredients in a stock pot. Bring the water to a boil. Lower the heat and simmer for approximately two hours or until the beans are tender. Add additional water if the beans become too dry. Before serving, season to taste with salt and pepper.

Rio Ranch
Houston

Crispy Chicken and Potato Tacos with Spicy Green Salsa

Makes 8 tacos

Tacos

4	ounces chicken breast, cooked and diced
1	Idaho potato, boiled, peeled and grated
4	ounces Monterey Jack cheese, grated
¼	white onion, diced
1	teaspoon salt
¼	teaspoon black pepper
20	fresh oregano leaves
8	corn tortillas
8	tooth picks
2	cups vegetable oil for frying

Combine the cooked chicken, potato, Monterey Jack cheese, onion, salt, pepper, and oregano and mix well.

Heat the oil in a heavy 10-inch skillet to 325°. Soft fry each tortilla for a few seconds on each side. The tortillas should not be crisp. Drain the fried tortillas on a paper towel. Reserve the oil in the skillet.

Arrange the filling along the diameter of each tortilla. Roll each tortilla around the filling to form a cylinder and fix with a toothpick.

Heat the oil to 325°. Fry two or three tacos at a time until the tortillas are crisp. Transfer the fried tacos to a paper towel. Allow to cool for about 10 minutes. Remove the toothpicks, then serve with the Spicy Salsa.

Spicy Salsa

6	tomatillos, husks removed and washed
¼	white onion, chopped
2	cloves garlic
1	serrano chile, stem removed
1	ripe avocado, peeled, seeded, and finely diced
1	tablespoon fresh cilantro, chopped
1	teaspoon lime juice
1	teaspoon salt
	Pinch black pepper

Combine the tomatillos, onion, garlic, and serrano chile in a sauce pan. Add enough water to cover the ingredients. Bring to a boil, then simmer for 5 minutes or until the tomatillos are soft. Discard the liquid and cool the ingredients.

Transfer the boiled ingredients to a blender and puree. Transfer the puree to a mixing bowl. Add the remaining ingredients and mix well.

Thelma Meltzer
Houston

Sainthood Soup

I love soup—to eat, to drink, even more to make—from a precise recipe (which I somehow always "adapt" a little (or even a lot) from scratch, making it up as I go along. This soup has no formal recipe—just ingredients you can change every time you make it, if you wish. Make it vegetarian or add the meat and broth of your choice.

I began making it for a friend who was in a long struggle with cancer, and changed it somewhat almost every time I made it for her. At one point a couple of years ago, she called to tell me she had dubbed it, "Yes, You Do Now Qualify for Sainthood" Soup. The ingredient I threw into that batch for the first time was butternut squash. It gave a distinctively different flavor. Later, I added the Thai herbs, lemon grass, and keiffer lime, and again it was different.

Whenever I make it, I throw in any vegetable I wish to—or herb too, for that matter. This is a "have fun with it" recipe, and the results will win you friends and influence people. Our daughter, Nancy, as a result of this new soup in the land, made a large tile wall plaque for me with two antique soup ladles hanging from it that spelled out in tile "Thelma, the Patron Saint of Soups."

Basic Recipe

	Chicken thighs or turkey necks
2 or 3	baking potatoes, peeled and diced
6	carrots, chopped
4	stalks celery, sliced
2	medium-size zucchini, diced
1 or 2	large shallots or 1 onion, chopped
1	can vegetable broth
1	medium butternut squash, peeled, cut in pieces, cooked
	basil to taste
	parsley
	Janee's Crazy Salt or salt and white pepper to taste
	Half-and-half milk or 2 percent milk, if you're calorie conscious

Cook meat with shallots or onions in one pot with water. In another large pot, cook potatoes, carrots, celery, and zucchini with water to cover, abut 20–25 minutes. Cool, peel, and add to other vegetables. When all are nearly done, add herbs, salt and pepper. Also at this time, you can add chopped lemon grass stalks and 2 or 3 Keiffer lime leaves. Pour off almost all liquid into a container. Mash vegetables with potato masher so they are small but still separate bits. Cut meat into bite-size pieces and add as much as you wish. Add chicken broth (canned, if you like) and as much vegetable liquid as you wish. Add half-and-half or 2 percent milk.

Sometimes I add a little chunk of margarine or butter. If the soup is thinner than you'd like, cook and mash another potato and add to thicken. Taste as you go—that's part of the fun. Bon appetit! And I'm here for consultation, if you need me.

The Herbs

The herbs described in this section are presented in alphabetical sequence. Though some of the herbs are of the same genus, they're quite different in culture, appearance, and use. Thus, they are listed individually; i.e, pennyroyal, a member of the mint family, is listed separately. An "A" following an herb's common and latin name designates it an annual; a "B" means biennial and a "P" perennial. Full sun means sun all day; partial shade refers to more sun than shade. Only a few herbs will survive in complete shade. With the exception of a few, I have grown every herb discussed in the pages that follow.

ALOE (Aloe vera) P

Propagation: By vegetative offshoots
  from the mother plant

Width & Height: 1' × 2'

Soil: Average to slightly sandy

Exposure: Full sun or partial shade

Water: Average

Aloe vera leaves, a few inches wide and up to 2 feet long, form a gray-green rosette. The center stem reaches a height of about 4 feet. Flowers form in a spectacular yellow-orange cluster almost a foot in length. Along the Gulf Coast (zones 9 and 10), aloes can reach 4 feet in height and get almost as wide. Don't confuse the agaves (century plants) with the aloes. Aloes have soft, pulpy leaves, while the agaves have stringy, tough leaves.

Culture. Aloes need a well-drained, moderately rich soil and do best with partial shade. They dislike wet feet and an excess of nitrogen.

The leaves of the aloe vera contain a mucilaginous substance soothing to minor skin irritations, abrasions, and burns.

Uses. I have seen ads extolling the aloe's virtues as an ingredient in cosmetics, but its prime use is medicinal. The juice from the leaves is used to treat burns, abrasions, and minor skin diseases. It is also very effective for sunburn. You can save the leaf you've used by covering it with plastic wrap and storing in your freezer till you need it again. Your plant will heal itself, sealing off the break in the leaf.

Remarks. The aloe is native to South Africa but is quite common to the arid regions of the United States, Mexico, and the Mediterranean (there are more than 200 varieties). They do quite well on a sunny windowsill indoors, and weekly watering with minimum fertilizing will make an attractive plant. Would you believe they belong to the lily family? They do, and so do the onion, tulip, and asparagus, but don't use these on the burns. Enjoy the beauty of the tulips, and eat the asparagus and onions.

ANGELICA (Angelica archangelica) P

Propagation: Seed

Width & Height: 2′ × 5′

Soil: Average

Exposure: Full sun or partial shade

Water: Frequent

This large, handsome plant can get to be 6 feet high and almost 3 feet wide. The leaf stems are unusual in appearance in that they start as a sort of sheath, developing into a compound five-segment leaf. Leaves can reach 5 inches or more in length and almost as wide. Green flowers are in rounded clusters and rise several feet above the main foliage of the plant.

Culture. Angelica likes average moist soil and cooler climates. It does best in the eastern portions of zones 7 and 8.

Uses. An oil is extracted from the leaves and roots for use in the manufacture of perfumes. This oil is also used to flavor liqueurs. Leaves and stalks can be eaten as a salad.

Remarks. Because the herb gets so tall, make sure it's in the background of your garden. Culpeper tells us this herb is good for "deafness, toothaches, and bites of mad dogs." Well, . . . maybe.

ANISE (Pimpinella anisum) A

Propagation: Seed

Width & Height: 1′ × 2′

Soil: Average

Exposure: Full sun

Water: Average

The leaves of anise are lobed and finely cut, with small white flowers developing in flat clusters. Plants can reach 2 feet in height and should be thinned 8 to 12 inches apart.

Culture. A well-drained, moderately rich soil in a sunny location.

Uses. The fresh leaves are used in salads, and the seeds in bread, cake, soup, and as a medicinal tea. Commercial uses include soap, perfume, tea, dental preparations, and flavoring for cough drops and liqueurs.

Remarks. Anise does well as a companion plant with coriander. Anise has a long taproot, and so it resents transplanting, but it's no problem if you've grown your plants in containers and then transfer them to the garden.

(Sweet) BASIL (Ocimum basilicum) A

Propagation: Seed

Width & Height: 2′ × 2′

Soil: Average

Exposure: Full sun

Water: Average

   The most common of the basils, sweet basil is a medium-size bushy plant reaching 2 feet in width and height. The leaves are 2 inches long and 1 inch wide, with a clove-pepperish taste and odor. There are many varieties of basil: the large-leaf plant reaches 3 feet tall; lettuce leaf, a Japanese basil, is a large plant with sawtooth leaves 4 inches long that resemble a leaf of lettuce. Sacred basil has an unusual fragrance and reaches 18 inches in height; and lemon basil, an unusual variety, is my favorite. Purple ruffles is probably the most striking with large crinkly purple leaves tinged with green. The lower leaves are almost a golden color. These leaves grow up to 3 inches long and half as wide. The herb can be used just like regular green basil. A close relative to this plant is green ruffles basil. The plant is a bit larger, but the leaves are the same size as purple ruffles. Opal basil has beautifully colored purple leaves.

   Another variety is spicy globe basil that grows as a perfect round clump about 18 inches across and half as tall. It looks like it was pruned to its perfect shape, but nature did that for you. The leaves are rounded and are the size of my five-year-old granddaughter's fingernail.

Basil is an easy herb to grow; it does well with minimal watering. Our warm southern climate forces basil to seed prolifically after flowering, so look for volunteer seedlings each fall.

Licorice basil leaves have a very unique fragrance. You guessed right, they smell like licorice. The plant is a bit over 16 inches tall and half as wide, with leaves a couple inches long and an inch wide. You can use a few leaves at a time in a salad or add some to the pesto you're making.

All these basils can be used as a garnish, and the plants should be available at your favorite nursery.

Culture. Basil is grown from seed in the spring and germinates in seven to ten days. Seedlings are easily transplanted. A light, well-drained medium rich soil in full sun is a good environment for this herb. Fertilize lightly after a moderate pruning. You can extend the life of your plant if you don't allow it to flower. So pinch off the seed heads.

Uses. This versatile flavoring herb enhances soups, stews, salads, cottage cheese, pesto, and many other foods. My wife uses the leaves in conjunction with other herbs to flavor roasting chicken, and, I might add, her chicken is a gourmet's delight. Basil's prime commercial use is in perfumes.

Remarks. Basil is a very easy herb to grow, and it manages very well with minimum water. The bush and opal varieties make lovely border plants requiring little or no care. In most of Texas, with over six months of warm weather, a flowering basil plant drops many seeds, resulting in many volunteer plants.

(Sweet) BAY (Laurus nobilis) P

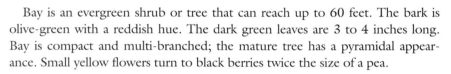

Propagation: Seed or cuttings

Width & Height: 5' × 10'

Soil: Average

Exposure: Full sun or partial shade

Water: Average

Bay is an evergreen shrub or tree that can reach up to 60 feet. The bark is olive-green with a reddish hue. The dark green leaves are 3 to 4 inches long. Bay is compact and multi-branched; the mature tree has a pyramidal appearance. Small yellow flowers turn to black berries twice the size of a pea.

Culture. Average well-drained soil, in either full or filtered sun. This is a slow plant to propagate, as are most trees. It takes four to six months to root cuttings, and seed viability (ability to germinate) is low, averaging about 25 percent.

This is a seedling of bay, a classic for all savory dishes.
This plant will become a tree up to 60' high.

Uses. Bay is used to flavor poultry, fish, pasta, and sweet dishes. Try a leaf in a pot of beans. Leaves can be used fresh or dry.

Remarks. Bay is hardy to 10° and can be grown outdoors in zones 8, 9, and 10. It makes a fine potted plant or hedge and can be pruned to any size.

BEE BALM (Monarda didyma) P

Propagation: Seed, cuttings, or division

Width & Height: 2' × 3'

Soil: Average

Exposure: Full sun

Water: Average

Bee balm is a bushy plant to 3 feet in height. Leaves are up to 6 inches long. Flowers are in dense clusters in red, pink, purple, or white, depending on variety.

Culture. Sun to partial shade in moist, slightly acid soil.

Uses. Used for tea, to flavor jellies, in fruit salads, and in potpourri.

Remarks. Commonly known as Oswego tea or bergamot, bee balm is native to the northeastern U.S., though some subspecies are natives of Texas. It is hardy to −20° and does quite well in all zones. The middle of the plant has a tendency to rot, so use outer shoots and roots when you propagate by division.

BORAGE (Borago officinalis) A

Propagation: Seed

Width & Height: 1' × 2'

Soil: Average

Exposure: Full sun or partial shade

Water: Minimum

This plant can reach 3 feet tall. The gray-green leaves are covered with bristly hairs and get up to 6 inches long. Borage has lovely blue star-shaped flowers that tend to droop downward.

Culture. Soil can be somewhat poor and on the dry side. Too much moisture will kill this plant. Borage does well in sun or partial shade.

Uses. The leaves have a cucumber-like flavor and are used in salads or cooked as greens. The flowers can be candied or used in iced drinks.

Remarks. Borage is an excellent bee plant. Culpeper tells us that it's a useful antidote for the venom of serpents. Nitrate of potash is one of the chemicals in this plant, and when burned it spews sparks with a slight explosive sound.

BURNET (Sanguisorba minor) P

Propagation: Seed or root division

Width & Height: 2' × 2'

Soil: Average

Exposure: Full sun

Water: Average

A bushy, full plant with lacy leaves, burnet reaches a height of up to 2 feet. The leaves are serrated in opposite pairs along the stalks. It is hardy to −25° and is evergreen in all zones.

Culture. Does well in average soil in full sun. In the North it takes a few years for a well-established plant; here in Texas, one growing season produces a vigorous, healthy plant.

Uses. Burnet has a fresh cucumber flavor and the leaves can be used in salads, iced drinks, cream cheese, and as a garnish.

Remarks. Makes a nice low hedge requiring minimum care. It is native to England and Europe and was brought to this country by the early settlers.

CAMOMILE (Anthemis nobilis) P

Propagation: Seed, root division, or
   layering

Width & Height: ½' × 1'

Soil: Sandy

Exposure: Full sun or partial shade

Water: Average

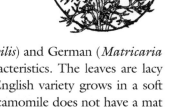

There are two varieties, English (*Anthemis nobilis*) and German (*Matricaria camomilla*) with both herbs having similar characteristics. The leaves are lacy with small flowers very similar to a daisy. The English variety grows in a soft mat, with flowers reaching a foot high. German camomile does not have a mat appearance but has delicate foliage surrounding the daisy-like flowers.

Culture. Camomile likes full or partial sun and a moist sandy soil.

Uses. The blossoms are used as a hair rinse for blondes. The dried blossoms make a mild tea. The oil is used in perfumes.

Remarks. The German variety flowers in a shorter period than does the English, and it self-sows throughout the year in zones 9 and 10. In mild winters, I have German camomile blooming all year.

CARAWAY (Carurm carvi) B

Propagation: Seed

Width & Height: 1' × 3'

Soil: Average

Exposure: Full sun

Water: Average

Caraway is a hardy biennial that sets seed the second year. This 2-foot plant has lacy foliage similar to carrots and does very well in southern gardens. The umbels, or seed heads, are creamy-white in color and reach 5 or 6 inches in diameter.

Culture. Sow in light soil, spacing so mature plants are a foot apart. Caraway has a long taproot and so is difficult to transplant. It's no problem grown in its own container and then set out in the garden, though.

Uses. The leaf is used in salads and soups. Caraway seeds, a favorite in German cooking, are used to flavor rye bread, cake, sauerkraut, baked apples, goulash, and soup. It's used commercially for perfume, liqueurs, and soap.

Remarks. In Texas, seeds can be planted in early fall and the plants will set seed heads the following summer. Broadcast seeds throughout the garden rather than restrict them to a bed. To have an appreciable amount of seeds, you need 40 to 50 plants. Seeds need to be harvested just before they are ripe or the wind will get most of them. Viability for seeds is several years; the fragrance improves with age.

Dioscorides advised pale-faced girls to partake of the oil. It was thought the seed would keep lovers from being fickle and would prevent fowl and pigeons from straying.

CATNIP (Nepeta cataria) P

Propagation: Seed, cuttings, or
  division

Width & Height: 3' × 2'

Soil: Average

Exposure: Full sun or partial shade

Water: Average

Catnip reaches 3 feet in height and can grow more than 4 feet wide. The gray heart-shaped leaves are up to 3 inches long. White flowers (with a lilt of purple) in dense clusters on spikes, make this a fine accent plant.

Culture. This herb does well in most any soil but will grow best in sandy soil. It self-sows, and plants are easily transplanted to other areas of the garden. Catnip does well in full or partial sun. It tends to get scraggly and needs to be pruned several times during the growing season.

Uses. Leaves make a hot tea that some drink to ease the discomfort of a cold. Large doses of warm tea induce vomiting. Catnip acts as a mild narcotic for most cats. Some cats enjoy fresh leaves; others prefer them dried. Leaves can be dried and sewn in a small sachet for your cat to play with.

Remarks. Protect your catnip until it's a foot tall—a cage of chicken wire is good. Your cat or your neighbor's can destroy a plant very quickly. My daughter's cat is not interested in catnip but prefers lemon grass, but what can you expect from a cat that drinks water from the faucet.

Rats avoid catnip. Either the odor is very disagreeable to them, they smell the recent presence of a feline, or experience has given them bad associations with the plant. Culpeper advises that catnip juice added to wine is good for bruises, whereas the tea applied to the head will heal sores.

CAYENNE (Capsicum minimum) P

Propagation: Seed

Width & Height: 1′ × 2′

Soil: Average

Exposure: Full sun or partial shade

Water: Average

There are many varieties of hot peppers (cayenne is just one), with pods ranging from 1 to 6 inches in length. It is perennial in its native tropical climates, but grows as an annual outside its native habitat. The leaves are half an inch wide and up to 2 inches long. The fruit, a seed pod, can be red, blue, yellow, or green. The plant grows up to 18 inches tall and wide.

Culture. Cayenne does well in most soils and in full or partial sun and doesn't require much care.

Use. An absolute must for flavoring Mexican food.

Remarks. Cayenne, with its many colorful pods, is an excellent border or accent plant. Peppers in your garden can be potted and brought indoors before the first freeze. There are many unusual varieties of hot peppers from Mexico. Regardless of what they look like, they all have the same hot flavor. Wash your hands thoroughly after handling this pungent herb.

CHERVIL (Anthriscus cerefolium) A

Propagation: Seed

Width & Height: 1′ × 2′

Soil: Sandy

Exposure: Partial shade

Water: Average

This annual reaches a height of up to 2 feet, with very lacy light green leaves. The flowers are delicate white in flat heads. Chervil resembles flat-leaf parsley, although it is a more dainty plant. It turns red in the late fall.

Culture. Chervil does best in well-drained soil with some shade. Plant close to taller herbs or vegetables to provide the necessary shade. Chervil self-sows, and in areas of Texas we can have several crops in a year.

Uses. There is a curled variety that has an anise flavor. The leaves are used in salads, soups, and as a garnish in much the same manner as parsley.

Remarks. A lovely, easy-care plant. The ancient Roman author Pliny advises that the seed taken in vinegar gets rid of hiccups.

CHIVES (Allium schoenoprasum) P

Propagation: Seed or division

Width & Height: ½′ × 1′

Soil: Average

Exposure: Full sun or partial shade

Water: Average

Chives are probably one of the most familiar and widely used herbs. This hardy perennial has small bulblets growing very close together in dense clusters. Its slender hollow leaves are cylindrical and grow to about 12 inches tall. The pale-purple flower heads are densely packed in a conical umbel. The small seeds are black and similar to onion seeds. As the plant gets larger, the leaves have a tendency to droop. This is normal for chives.

Garlic chives (*A. schoenoprasum* var. *sibricum*) have a mild garlic flavor. At maturity, garlic chives (Chinese chives, oriental chives) are the same size as a tubular chives plant. The flowers of the garlic variety are white and grow in attractive star-like clusters. This herb usually flowers in late July or early August.

Culture. Both varieties do well in any garden soil. Clumps should be divided into smaller clumps with eight or ten bulblets. You can cut your clump of chives several times a year. Fertilize after each cutting. Chives will not flower with continual pruning. If you use them as border plants, don't prune till the flowers have set seed.

Uses. Chives are great in salads, soups, and many other dishes. I take a handful of either variety and, with scissors, snip them into very small pieces. Mixing chives with scrambled eggs makes a very tasty breakfast dish.

Remarks. As members of the onion family, chives deter many harmful insects in the vegetable garden. I randomly plant both varieties in my garden.

COMFREY
(Symphytum officinale) P

Propagation: Root divisions

Width & Height: 2′ × 3′

Soil: Average

Exposure: Full sun

Water: Average

The main stem of comfrey is covered with bristly hairs and can reach 3 feet tall. Leaves on the lower part of the plant are largest (up to 10 inches long), decreasing in size as they grow up the stem. Like the stalk, the leaves are quite hairy and promote itching when handled. The drooping flowers, usually purple, bloom through the greater part of the summer. There are several varieties of comfrey, but *S. officinale* is the most common.

Cultivation. Comfrey does well in full or partial sun and in average soil. Plants should be spaced 3 feet apart. Several cuttings a year can be made from this perennial (it's hardy to −30°). It's a heavy nitrogen feeder and should be fertilized after each cutting.

Uses. This herb, rich in calcium, phosphorus, potassium, and high in protein, makes an excellent supplement for livestock and poultry. The young leaves can be used in salads, cooked as greens, in soups, or as a tea.

Aloe Vera

Angelica

Arugula

Sweet Basil

Purple Ruffles Basil

Cinnamon Basil

Bay

Borage

Burnet

Camomile

Chives

Comfrey

Comfrey and Costmary

Dill

Fennel

Elephant Garlic

Society Garlic

Rose Geranium

119

Lamb's Ear

English Lavender

Lemon Grass

Lemon Verbena

Lion's Ear

Luffa

120

Makrut

Apple Mint

Mexican Marigold Mint

Licorice Mint

Pineapple Mint

Ohja Santa

Thai Pepper

Jerusalem Sage

Rosemary

Golden Sage

Rose Campion

Mexican Sage

122

Southernwood

French Shallots

Pineapple Sage

Winter Savory

Santolina

French Sorrel

French Tarragon

Thyme

Violet

Wormwood

Golden Yarrow

White Yarrow

Comfrey produces drooping purple flowers that bloom throughout the summer.

Remarks. A small bit of root means another plant, so plant this herb where it will be happy for years to come. I'm sure a plant or two will be very happy off in a corner of your garden. I've been trying to reduce my 30 or so plants down to 10. It's very difficult, but I'm making some progress. Comfrey leaves are excellent for your compost pile. Allantoin, which promotes healing of cuts and lacerations, is a valuable component of comfrey. Culpeper tells us that comfrey is good for gout, ulcers, bruises, wounds, ruptures, and helps mend broken bones.

CORIANDER/CILANTRO
(Coriandrum sativum) A

Propagation: Seed

Width & Height: 1' × 2'

Soil: Average

Exposure: Full sun

Water: Average

The stem of coriander gets up to 3 feet tall and quite slender and branched. Leaves are almost round and slightly lobed. The flowers are off-

The Egyptians and Israelites used coriander over 2,500 years ago. Note the volunteer plants that have sprouted at the bottom of this large specimen.

white and complement the plant's bright green appearance. Seeds should be picked just before they are ripe or the wind will random plant them for you.

Culture. Coriander does well in any well-drained soil in full sun. It has a long taproot and is difficult to transplant. It's no problem if it's grown in its own container and then planted outdoors.

Uses. Flavors Mexican, Thai, Indian, and other international foods.

Remarks. The foliage and seeds of coriander have an unpleasant musty odor. They lose this odor when dry, and the seeds become more fragrant the drier they get. This herb is one of several used by the Egyptians and Israelites over 2,500 years ago.

COSTMARY
(Tanacetum balsamita) P

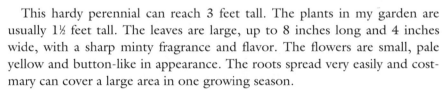

Propagation: Root division

Width & Height: 1′ × 2′

Soil: Average

Exposure: Full sun or partial shade

Water: Average

This hardy perennial can reach 3 feet tall. The plants in my garden are usually 1½ feet tall. The leaves are large, up to 8 inches long and 4 inches wide, with a sharp minty fragrance and flavor. The flowers are small, pale yellow and button-like in appearance. The roots spread very easily and costmary can cover a large area in one growing season.

Culture. This herb prefers full sun but will thrive in partial shade. It likes almost any soil as long as it's fairly dry and well-drained.

Uses. In England, costmary was used to flavor ale: "alecost" is another of its common names. It is used in salads and potpourri.

Remarks. In colonial days, churchgoers used costmary as markers for their Bibles, hence another common name, "Bible leaf."

DILL (Anethum graveolens) A

Propagation: Seed

Width & Height: 1' × 3'

Soil: Average

Exposure: Full sun

Water: Average

This hardy annual, similar in appearance to fennel, grows from 2½ to 3 feet tall. It usually has one stalk with sparse feathery leaves. The umbels, or flat seed heads, are 4 or 5 inches across. The flowers are a pretty yellow and add quite a bit of color when randomly planted in the garden. The entire plant is very aromatic.

Culture. Dill grows well in most any well-drained soil.

Uses. The seeds and leaves are used to flavor soups, sauces, fish, and in pickling cucumbers. The French flavor their cakes and pastries with dill seed.

Remarks. This native of the Mediterranean region was used as a drug in the 10th century. Magicians used it to combat witchcraft.

Be sure to clip the seedhead of dill just after it turns brown. Otherwise, the wind will scatter the seeds everywhere.

Culpeper tells us that it strengthens the brain, controls hiccups, and helps to expel "wind." Dill seeds should be collected when they first turn brown. If you neglect to collect them, it's only a matter of a few days before the wind random plants them for you.

DITTANY OF CRETE
(Amaracus dictamnus) P

Propagation: Seed, cuttings, or plant division

Width & Height: 1′ × 2′

Soil: Sandy

Exposure: Full sun

Water: Minimum

Dittany of Crete is a very ornamental plant with soft hairy gray leaves ½ inch long and wide. The slender stems grow about a foot long. The flowers are purple and quite small.

Culture. This herb does well with full sun, minimum watering, and sandy soil.

Uses. Dittany is a culinary herb for Greek and Italian cooking. The flowers are used for tea.

Remarks. This herb makes an excellent ground cover. It is fine for rock gardens and makes a spectacular hanging basket plant with its long leafy trailing stems.

ELECAMPANE
(Inula helenium) P

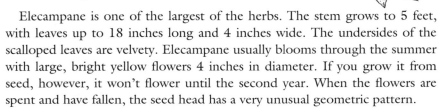

Propagation: Seed or root division

Width & Height: 2′ × 4′

Soil: Sandy

Exposure: Partial shade

Water: Frequent

Elecampane is one of the largest of the herbs. The stem grows to 5 feet, with leaves up to 18 inches long and 4 inches wide. The undersides of the scalloped leaves are velvety. Elecampane usually blooms through the summer with large, bright yellow flowers 4 inches in diameter. If you grow it from seed, however, it won't flower until the second year. When the flowers are spent and have fallen, the seed head has a very unusual geometric pattern.

Culture. It does best in moist, well-drained soil in partial shade.

Uses. Roots are candied for a cough medicine. In Europe the roots are used with wormwood foliage in the preparation of absinthe. It is given to horses to improve their coats.

Remarks. The 16th-century authors tell us this herb is good for fevers, the plague, and destroys worms in the stomach.

FENNEL (Foeniculum vulgare) P

Propagation: Seed

Width & Height: 2′ × 4′

Soil: Average

Exposure: Full sun

Water: Average

Fennel is a large herb, 4 or 5 feet tall, with a bright green, almost polished appearance. The leaves are feathery or lacy, very similar to the dill leaf.

Fennel is an excellent all-purpose kitchen herb. Use for garnishes, in salads and meats; the slender, white stalks can be eaten raw like celery.

Bright golden-yellow flowers adorn this plant. Florence fennel (*F. vulgare* var. *dulce*), also called finocchio, is an annual and a much smaller plant. It has a swollen base with white stalks. This annual reaches a height of 15 to 18 inches, with flowers similar to vulgare. It usually blooms earlier than the perennial variety.

Culture. Fennel is easily grown from seed, likes full sun, and does well in any well-drained soil. Florence fennel requires more watering and a richer soil.

Uses. The leaves are used for garnishes, in salads and puddings, and to flavor Italian sausage. The tender stems are soaked in water and eaten raw like celery. Seeds are used to flavor cordials and liqueurs. Fennel also makes a good tea.

Remarks. This native of temperate Europe and the Mediterranean has followed civilization, usually where Italians have traveled. In medieval times this plant was hung over the doors to keep away evil spirits. The ancient Greeks tell us that partaking of the herb increases the life span and gives strength and courage.

FOXGLOVE (Digitalis purpurea) B

Propagation: Seed; low germination
  percent

Width & Height: 1' × 4'

Soil: Average

Exposure: Full sun

Water: Frequent

Foxglove is classed as a biennial, but sometimes it can flower for several years. This handsome plant produces a flower stalk up to 4 feet tall. Large leaves, almost a foot long, grow at the base of the plant. The long bell-shaped flowers are 2 inches long and purple or white with speckled throats. The flowers are borne on stalks a few feet above the foliage.

Culture. Does best in rich, friable, moist soil in full sun.

Uses. Foxglove is a source of digitalis, a heart stimulant.

Remarks. The true medicinal plant has deep pink or magenta flowers; the pale-flowered variety does not produce the drug. This is a beautiful plant and should be grown for show.

GARLIC (Allium sativum) P

Propagation: By cloves from the bulb

Width & Height: 1' × 3'

Soil: Average

Exposure: Full sun

Water: Average

This 2-foot tall herb, in my opinion, belongs in every garden. The bulb consists of several cloves enclosed together in a thin white skin. The stem is smooth, surrounded at the bottom by tubular leaf sheaths from which the long, flat linear leaves grow. The flower umbel is at the top of the main stalk. The white flowers comprising the umbel are usually sterile.

A variety of garlic is called elephant garlic (*Allium ampeloprasum*). When you see the size of the bulb and cloves, you understand why it's called elephant. Some of the bulbs can exceed a pound. The flavor is sweeter and not as strong as regular garlic. I would suggest planting this herb in the autumn. It does better through our fall and mild winters. Usually it matures in 120–150 days.

Culture. Garlic does best in rich, sandy, moderately moist soil in full sun. Cloves should be planted, pointy end up, about 2 inches deep and 6 to 8 inches apart. Keep your garlic bed hoed and free of weeds. Mulching will help to conserve moisture and reduce weed growth. When the leaves dry and turn brown (after four to six months), the bulbs are ready to harvest, dry, and store.

Uses. Garlic contains a lot of vitamins, and is not only a healthful herb, but it adds zest and wonderful flavor to all the dishes it flavors. It is a widely used seasoning for many Italian dishes. It was used as an antiseptic during World War II. Research is currently in progress testing garlic for possible use in treating various cardiovascular diseases. A friend had a year-old dog in very poor health. She fed him a daily ration of garlic and it helped restore him to health in about 4 months.

SCENTED GERANIUM
(Pelargonium spp.) P

Propagation: Seed or cuttings

Width & Height: ½′ × 1′

Soil: Sandy

Exposure: Full sun or partial shade

Water: Minimum

Scented geraniums (*Pelargonium spp.*) comprise a very extensive genus. I'll give a general description of some of those I grow. Coconut-scented geranium has a round medium green leaf, about an inch or so across, with lovely tiny pink flowers. It's a trailing variety and has to be in a hanging basket, for it'll trail 2 feet down the sides. There's an apple-scented geranium that has small white flowers and also does well in a hanging basket; its leaves get as large as 2½ inches wide and long. Nutmeg-scented geranium, with

Among the various scented geraniums are an amazing array of fragrances: coconut, rose, apple, mint, cinnamon, lemon, lime, orange, and more. This nutmeg-scented geranium has delicate white flowers and makes a fine container specimen.

inch-long gray-green leaves and small white flowers makes a fine container plant. Cinnamon-scented has leaves an inch wide and long, also produces small white flowers, and is another nice pot plant. There is lemon-rose, which has very large, rounded leaves; rose-scented has large leaves that are more wrinkled than lemon. Attar of rose and crowsfoot are very similar in appearance, but the leaves on crowsfoot are more sharply cut back. Leaves of both species are so sharply divided that they appear fern-like; the flowers of both are a medium purple. Lemon-scented has small ¾-inch leaves, whereas lime-scented has very tiny crinkled leaves.

My favorite geranium is the peppermint-scented variety. The leaves are quite large (3 inches wide and long) and hairy. To me it has one of the most pungent fragrances of all the scented geraniums. All the rose species need at least a gallon-size container or larger, for they can reach 2 feet in height.

Culture. Sandy, well-drained soil, and at least 6 to 8 hours of sun a day. Geraniums like it a bit dry. If the lower leaves get yellow, you're overwatering. Purple leaves mean a lack of phosphorus. One-half a teaspoon of bonemeal sprinkled on the surface and watered in will remedy the deficiency.

Uses. Commercially, the fragrant oils are used in perfumes. The leaves flavor jellies, jams, custards, and puddings. Scented geraniums are also fine additions to potpourri.

Remarks. These herbs are very easy to grow and care for, and their exotic fragrances are a must for every home and garden. They do very well in containers or in the ground. Get some, you'll love them.

GERMANDER (Teucrium lucidum) P

Propagation: Seed, cuttings, or root
  division

Width & Height: 1½' × 1'

Soil: Average

Exposure: Full sun

Water: Minimum

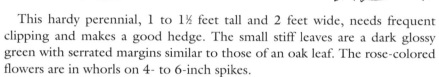

   This hardy perennial, 1 to 1½ feet tall and 2 feet wide, needs frequent clipping and makes a good hedge. The small stiff leaves are a dark glossy green with serrated margins similar to those of an oak leaf. The rose-colored flowers are in whorls on 4- to 6-inch spikes.

Culture. Germander does well in any well-drained soil in full sun with minimum care.

Uses. Years ago this herb, in conjunction with other herbs, was used as a cure for gout.

Remarks. The herbalists of the 15th and 16th centuries tell us that mixed in wine it's very effective against the poison of serpents and diseases of the brain. So, not only will it make a lovely hedge, but with a bottle of wine, you're protected from poisonous serpents in your backyard. Quite a number of the herbs, according to the ancient herbalists, are great as medicines to combat venomous serpents.

GINGER (Zingiber officinale) P

Propagation: By root or plant
  division

Width & Height: 1' × 2'

Soil: Average

Exposure: Full sun

Water: Average

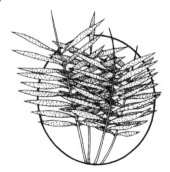

Ginger, a perennial root, grows and increases underground in tuberous joints. The stalk is approximately 2 feet high with several spikes of white or yellow blossoms. The leaves, 2 inches long and half as wide, have a very fragrant odor of—that's right—ginger.

Culture. My ginger grows in average garden soil in full sun. I've had to cut back the bed several times in past years.

Uses. Ginger is used as a condiment; medicinally, it is an aid in treatment of gastritis. A hot tea for relief of colds is also made from the roots.

Remarks. Jamaica and the West Indies cultivate and export most of the ginger used in the U.S. There is a wild ginger, *Asarum canadense*, native to North America and found in eastern portions of zone 7. This stemless perennial is a low, spreading, little plant that may reach 12 inches tall. The leaves are heart-shaped, with brown-purple drooping flowers. The entire plant has a strong ginger fragrance and was used by the North American Indians to cover up the smell of spoiled meat.

GINSENG (Panax quinquefolium) P

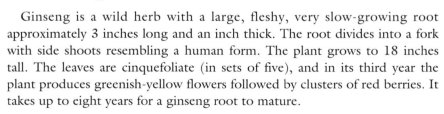

Propagation: Seed

Width & Height: 1′ × 1½′

Soil: Average

Exposure: Partial shade

Water: Average

Ginseng is a wild herb with a large, fleshy, very slow-growing root approximately 3 inches long and an inch thick. The root divides into a fork with side shoots resembling a human form. The plant grows to 18 inches tall. The leaves are cinquefoliate (in sets of five), and in its third year the plant produces greenish-yellow flowers followed by clusters of red berries. It takes up to eight years for a ginseng root to mature.

Culture. Ginseng grows best in light, well-drained, rich soil in the woods on protected north slopes.

Uses. This herb is prized by the Chinese, who consider it a remedy for most diseases.

Remarks. I have seen many ads telling how much money you can make growing and selling ginseng. Balderdash! As I said above, it takes several years and absolutely perfect growing conditions for roots large enough to sell. Incidentally, these people will sell you seed (rather expensive) and a book (also expensive). If you want to experiment, that's fine, but don't plan to realize many dollars from your ginseng farm.

HOREHOUND
(Marrubium vulgare) P

Propagation: Seed, cuttings, or root division

Width & Height: 6′ × 1½′

Soil: Average

Exposure: Full sun

Water: Minimum

Horehound usually is no more than 2 feet tall, but it can reach 6 feet in width. The leaves are very wrinkled and are covered with white hairs. The stem becomes woody in a year-old plant. The flowers, off-white in color, are small and inconspicuous.

Culture. Does well in poor soil in full sun.

Uses. Its prime use is for horehound candy used for coughs and colds. In England this herb is the ingredient for horehound ale, reputed to be a very healthful beverage.

Remarks. Here's another herb that ancient herbalists say was good for the bite of serpents—and mad dogs too! Black horehound (*M. nigrum*) is distinguished by its foul odor. It is a very unattractive plant.

Horehound has distinctly furrowed leaves. It is used to brew ale and to flavor candies.

HORSERADISH
(Armoracia rusticana) P

Propagation: Root division

Width & Height: 1′ × 2′

Soil: Average

Exposure: Full sun

Water: Average

The root of horseradish (the portion used for flavoring) reaches deeply into the soil, branching in all directions. Roots are long and cylindrical, with a cream-colored skin and white flesh. The leaves are very large, up to 14 inches long and 5 to 6 inches wide. The plant usually attains a height of 18 to 24 inches. The flowers are white with a green cast, on a stalk not much taller than the plant.

Culture. This herb grows best in a rich, well-drained soil, but it will develop a fair root system in dry soil. Plant it off in a corner. When you dig your roots late in the fall, you must get every bit of root, for any bit of root left in the ground means another plant next spring.

Uses. The roots are grated and used as condiment for seafood and meat. Horseradish is one of the bitter herbs the Jews eat at the Passover. It is a powerful stimulant and an excellent aid in digestion. My mother made horseradish, and one taste would make you gasp and bring tears to your eyes. Horseradish is also a rich source of vitamin C.

HYSSOP
(Hyssopus officinalis) P

Propagation: Seed, cuttings, or plant
   division

Width & Height: 1' × 1'

Soil: Sandy

Exposure: Full sun

Water: Minimum

This evergreen shrub reaches 1 to 2 feet high and is a very attractive border plant. It has dark foliage and flowering spikes of pink, white, or blue, depending on the variety. The small leaves, a dark green, have a sharp taste and a fragrance reminiscent of sage. The flowers have a spicy balsam odor.

Culture. Hyssop does best in dry, sandy soil in full sun.

Uses. The oil is used in perfumes, and a tea is made from the leaves and stems to treat rheumatism. It also is used as an ingredient in liqueurs.

Remarks. This herb is mentioned frequently in the Old Testament: David mentions it in a prayer, and Moses tells the Israelites to dip hyssop in the blood of a lamb.

LAMB'S EAR (Stachys lantana) P

Propagation: Seed or plant division

Width & Height: 1' × 1'

Soil: Sandy

Exposure: Full sun

Water: Minimum

This hardy perennial is a foot tall with soft, downy long linear gray leaves up to 3 inches long and half as wide. When stroked gently, the leaves feel like a lamb's ear. The entire plant has an almost silvery appearance. Most of the leaves grow from the root, and the purple flowers grow on a long stalk, rising a foot or so above the plant.

Culture. Lamb's ear likes full sun and a sandy soil. As this plant increases in size and the leaves touch and cover the ground it becomes a breeding place for pill bugs. Periodically, gently lift the lower leaves around the entire plant and brush the bugs out. They can destroy a well-established plant.

Uses. The dried leaves make a tea to relieve headaches and calm the nerves.

Remarks. I've read that the juice can be used to heal cuts and old sores. I'm old, so I presume it will heal any sores I have.

LAVENDER (Lavandula spp.) P

Propagation: Seed or cuttings

Width & Height: 1' × 2'

Soil: Sandy

Exposure: Full sun

Water: Minimum

There are many varieties of lavender, with the most common and largest being *L. spica,* or English lavender. Depending on the variety, this herb

Flowering French lavender needs full sun and sandy well-drained soil.

ranges from 1 to 4 feet tall and up to 3 feet across. It is a woody plant and has very fragrant flowers, usually lavender or deep purple in color. The narrow gray leaves are 2 inches long and make lovely contrasting plants with the predominant greens of other herbs. In addition to a number of dwarf varieties of lavender, there are Spanish (*L. Stoechas*), French (*L. dentata*), and spike lavender (*L. Lafifolia*), all approximately the same size as English lavender.

Culture. All lavenders need full sun, a sandy well-drained soil, and I suggest a raised bed to improve drainage. Most varieties need winter protection in zones 7 and 8.

Uses. Fragrant oils of lavender are used in toilet water, soap, perfume, and the blossoms for potpourri.

Remarks. It takes 60 pounds of flowers to produce 16 ounces of oil. This is another herb used as an antidote for the bites of mad dogs and serpents.

LEMON BALM
(Melissa officinalis) P

Propagation: Seed, cuttings, or plant
  division

Width & Height: 1' × 3'

Soil: Average

Exposure: Full sun or partial shade

Water: Minimum

The stem of lemon balm is upright and hairy with ovate, opposite leaves. The light- to dark-green leaves are 2–3 inches long with scalloped edges. The leaves at the base of the stem are largest, diminishing in size toward the top of the plant. The flowers are usually sparse, white, and quite small. The leaves, when bruised, have a strong lemon odor.

Culture. Lemon balm does well in most well-drained soils, in full sun or partial shade. It tends to wilt during extended dry spells (which do occur here in the South, in spite of all our rain). Pruning is necessary to keep this plant in bounds; it can be cut back any time of the year.

Uses. This herb makes an excellent tea and a garnish for fish. The oil is used as a base for perfume and for furniture polish. Dry leaves are used in potpourri.

Remarks. The name *Melissa* is from the Greek word for bee. Dioscorides, a Greek physician in the first century, said that lemon balm can be used as a remedy against the bite of a mad dog by steeping the leaves in wine, drinking it, and also applying the leaves externally. Lemon balm tea, according to one 15th-century herbalist, is good for female complaints. If your wife complains, about anything, fix her a cup of tea and advise me of the results.

LEMON GRASS
(Cynbopogon citratus) P

Propagation: Plant division

Width & Height: 1' × 2'

Soil: Average

Exposure: Full sun

Water: Average

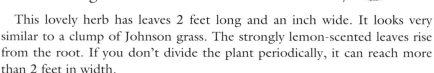

This lovely herb has leaves 2 feet long and an inch wide. It looks very similar to a clump of Johnson grass. The strongly lemon-scented leaves rise from the root. If you don't divide the plant periodically, it can reach more than 2 feet in width.

Culture. Lemon grass does well in full or partial sun and with average watering. It is hardy in zone 10 but needs winter protection in zone 9. It can manage 20° weather with 8 to 10 inches of mulch. When you divide the plant for propagation, cut off all but a few inches of leaves, making sure that each small clump has some root system.

Uses. Its prime use is in the manufacture of perfume. In my opinion, it makes one of the tastiest herb teas. It is also used to flavor Oriental dishes.

Lemon grass, a very tropical-looking herb, makes a delicious tea.

Remarks. This native of the tropical climes is grown commercially in India and Ceylon. This is one of the many scented grasses that include *C. nardus* grown in Ceylon, Java, and Burma, and *C. martine* grown in India.

LEMON TREE
(Eucalyptus citriodora) P

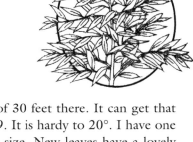

Propagation: Seed or cuttings

Width & Height: 3′ × 10′

Soil: Average

Exposure: Full sun

Water: Average

   This Australian native will reach a height of 30 feet there. It can get that tall in zone 10, and perhaps 10 feet in zone 9. It is hardy to 20°. I have one about 5 feet tall that I keep pruned to bush size. New leaves have a lovely almost iridescent color. As the tree grows, the leaves become a medium green. The spear-shaped leaves have a lovely lemon scent and are 4 to 5 inches long and an inch wide.

Culture. I'm growing my tree in full sun in compost-enriched soil. It looks quite pretty pruned to a bush.

Uses. The oil distilled from the leaves is used to make perfume. This citron-scented gum tree contains up to 98 percent of citronellol, a prime ingredient for perfumery.

Remarks. The genus Eucalyptus contains over 300 species native to Australia and Tasmania. They grow very quickly, and one of the tallest known trees is *E. Amygdalin,* which attains a height of almost 500 feet.

LEMON VERBENA
(Lippia citriodora) P

Propagation: Seed or cuttings

Width & Height: 2' × 4'

Soil: Average

Exposure: Full sun

Water: Average

Lemon verbena, in my opinion, is "Queen of the Herbs." This leafy shrub can reach a height of 10 to 12 feet in zone 10. It is an excellent pot plant, and in a 10-gallon container it can grow to 6 feet tall. The leaves, up to 5 inches long and less than an inch wide, are a shiny light green. They are slightly rough to the touch, with a delightful lemon fragrance. The flowers are very small, purple and white, and grow in slim terminal spikes.

Culture. Lemon verbena likes full sun and average well-drained garden soil.

Uses. The leaves are used for tea, perfume, and to flavor jellies. A few leaves in water make a fragrant finger bowl for the dinner table.

Lemon verbena can grow to 6' tall. Its redolent lemon fragrance is one of the most delightful of all.

Remarks. The leaves dry very quickly, usually in a week, spread out on a newspaper in the open shade. This herb needs winter protection in zones 8 and 9.

LUFFA (Lufa aegyptica) A

Propagation: Seeds

Width & Height: This vine runs 15′–20′ horizontally and 3′ high

Soil: Average

Exposure: Full sun

Water: Average

This annual plant does best along a chain link or similar open fence. The plant, like cucumbers, sends out little vines that attach themselves to the fence as the vine grows. If you grow along a wooden fence, these little vines need to be attached to the fence. Another alternative would be to loosely attach several strings a foot apart along the wood fence. The plants can easily grow 15 or 20 feet in a growing season.

Culture. Luffa likes the full sun, and average watering and fertilizing will produce many fruits until the first freeze.

Remarks. The bright yellow flowers become a small edible fruit, and if allowed to grow, reach up to 2 feet long and 3–4 inches thick. Most fruit will be about 16 inches long. These large gourds make an excellent body sponge for shower or tub as well as a scrubber for pots and pans. Dirty ones, that is. If planted in late March, some of the fruit will be large enough to pick in late July. The plant will produce fruit until the first freeze. Pick the fruit when the skin is slightly yellow. Squeeze hard with both hands to break the skin. Do this many times to make it easier to peel off the skin. Rinse several times; a hose is easiest. Squeeze out the excess water and set in the open shade to dry. When dry, shake out the seeds and save them for next year. Save only the black ones. There are many seeds in each fruit, and enough to supply all your neighbors.

Another method of removing the skin is to boil the luffas. You'll need a large pot, of course. After about 30 minutes of boiling, allow to cool and then peel off the skin. This method results in a very light colored (cream) sponge. The seeds must be discarded.

I have left fruit on the vine till it turns brown, and then peeled off the skin. The seeds are fine to save, and you don't need to rinse the gourd. The sponge will be darker, a light brown.

MARJORAM
(Marjorana hortensis) P

Propagation: Seed or cuttings

Width & Height: 3′ × 1′

Soil: Average

Exposure: Full sun

Water: Average

This fragrant herb can reach 18 inches in height and 3 to 4 feet across. The stems tend to get woody, and the small oval leaves are light green in color on top, with the underside having a gray-green cast. The flowers, white in color, grow in small tight clusters.

Culture. Sweet marjoram does well in most soils in full sun.

Uses. We are all familiar with marjoram as a culinary seasoning. The oil is used in soap and perfume.

Remarks. It takes in excess of 200 pounds of leaves to produce 16 ounces of oil. It was the custom of Greeks and Romans to make a crown of sweet marjoram for newlyweds. American colonists used the oil on furniture.

MEXICAN MARIGOLD MINT
(Tagetes lucidia) P

Propagation: Seed, cuttings, or plant division

Width & Height: 1' × 2'

Soil: Average

Exposure: Full sun

Water: Average

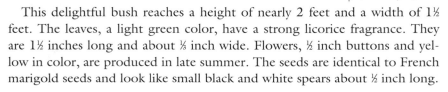

This delightful bush reaches a height of nearly 2 feet and a width of 1½ feet. The leaves, a light green color, have a strong licorice fragrance. They are 1½ inches long and about ⅛ inch wide. Flowers, ½ inch buttons and yellow in color, are produced in late summer. The seeds are identical to French marigold seeds and look like small black and white spears about ½ inch long.

Culture. Full sun means a very tight bushy plant; they tend to get scraggly in partial shade. I have this herb growing in several types of soil: sandy compost—enriched, and heavy. They all do well with average watering.

Uses. The leaves make an unusual tea and are a great substitute for French tarragon.

Mexican marigold mint has a strong licorice fragrance. Try in potpourri.

Remarks. Mexican marigold mint makes a lovely low hedge, a planting against the house, or out in your herb garden. Hardy in zone 9; winter protect in zone 8.

MINT (Mentha spp.) P

Propagation: Seed, cuttings, or plant
  division

Width & Height: 3′ × 1′

Soil: Average

Exposure: Full sun or partial shade

Water: Average to frequent

There are three important species of mint: peppermint, spearmint, and pennyroyal. The latter is discussed separately. Spearmint, probably the most common, has a bright green wrinkled leaf with serrated edges. The leaves are an inch to 1½ inches long and are half as wide. The erect stems reach 2 feet in height, and in mid-summer the entire plant is covered with tiny pink flowers in a circular pattern around the upper leaves. Wrigley's spearmint, with a fragrance of its own, is very similar to spearmint except that this vari-

Spearmint has bright green wrinkled leaves with serrated edges.

ety has leaves that are more rounded. Once you've seen and smelled both mints, there's no mistake as to the proper identification.

In the peppermint group, blackstem peppermint is probably the most common. The dark green leaves are an inch long and half an inch wide and are shaped like an arrowhead with a blunted point. Violet flowers are in cylindrical clusters near the upper leaves. The stems reach approximately a foot in height. Mild peppermint is quite different in appearance, fragrance, and size. The leaves of this plant are up to 2 inches long and only ½ inch wide. Stalks can reach over 2 feet tall.

Pineapple mint, with its varigated leaves, is a very striking plant. Apple mint with its large, almost round, very hairy leaf is another fragrant member of the Mentha family. Another varigated mint is golden mint. This is the last mint to produce foliage in the spring. It's less than a foot tall, with beautifully variegated yellowish-gold and green leaves. Orange mint, or bergamot, has purple-tinged leaves and a citrus fragrance. Probably the largest mint leaves in my garden belong to red-stem apple mint. The leaves are up to 3 inches long and 1½ inches wide. The erect reddish-tinged stems reach a height of 2 feet.

Corsican mint rarely gets over an inch tall and grows in a dense mat. Its tiny leaves and purple flowers are lovely in a rock garden. I have a water mint, a native of Oregon, that a friend brought me several years ago. It has a smooth rounded leaf and the stem is 18 inches tall.

Another variety is licorice mint. It has a strong licorice fragrance. It makes an excellent tea.

Culture. Mints like moisture and do quite well in full and partial sun. They'll grow in most any soil, but will do best in rich, friable soil. Roots need to be dug up to restrict the bed or mint can take over your entire garden. It likes a balanced fertilizer on a periodic basis.

Uses. Mint's prime use is culinary, but the oils are used in many other items such as shampoo, fragrant sprays, toothpaste, and in some medicines that have an otherwise unpleasant taste.

Remarks. The Greeks and Romans used mint to add fragrance to their baths. The mint was a highly esteemed herb; this herb was a tithe to the rulers of Egypt.

MUGWORT (Artemisia vulgaris) P

Propagation: Seed or cuttings

Width & Height: 3′ × 2′

Soil: Average

Exposure: Full sun

Water: Average

Mugwort can get as tall as 3 feet, sprawling to 4 feet in width. The smooth, dark green leaves are slightly lobed, and have a feathery delicate look. The flowers are in small oval-shaped patterns and are red or yellow. It's an unusual looking plant, and when pruned properly, it's very graceful.

Culture. My mugwort does quite well in full sun in average well-drained garden soil.

Uses. In the early 1900s, when tea was expensive in England, many people brewed tea from the leaves. It is used as a culinary herb in Europe. It is taken as a warm infusion with pennyroyal and southernwood leaves at the first sign of a cold.

Remarks. The ancient herbalists used this herb for hysterics, to kill worms, and to treat ailments of the liver.

Properly trimmed, mugwort makes an interesting, graceful low hedge.

NASTURTIUM (Tropaeolum spp.) P

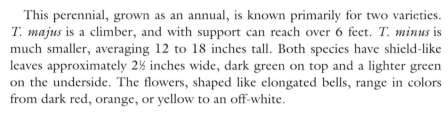

Propagation: Seed

Width & Height: 1' × 2'

Soil: Sandy

Exposure: Full sun

Water: Average

   This perennial, grown as an annual, is known primarily for two varieties. *T. majus* is a climber, and with support can reach over 6 feet. *T. minus* is much smaller, averaging 12 to 18 inches tall. Both species have shield-like leaves approximately 2½ inches wide, dark green on top and a lighter green on the underside. The flowers, shaped like elongated bells, range in colors from dark red, orange, or yellow to an off-white.

Culture. Several hours of sun a day in sandy soil is a good environment for this herb. Too rich a soil will produce lush foliage but not many flowers.

Uses. It has been used as a dye plant, in perfumes, and the leaves and flowers in salads.

Remarks. Nasturtium should be planted around the roots of your squash plants to repel the squash bug.

OREGANO (Origanum vulgare) P

Propagation: Seed, cuttings, or plant
   division

Width & Height: 1' × 2'

Soil: Average

Exposure: Full sun or partial shade

Water: Average

   This 2-foot-tall native of Europe spreads by invasive underground runners. The stems are very leafy, with flat clusters of small pink blossoms at the end of the stem. The leaves are an inch long, hairy, and medium-green in color. Greek oregano (*O. prismaticm*) is very similar to vulgare, having a slightly different flavor and brown flowers. It spreads more rapidly, covering a large area in one growing season. I have another variety called *Origanum majorana*. It has a perfume-like fragrance and is evergreen in South Texas. Like the *vulgare,* it can spread quite a bit in a growing season. The leaves are smaller, and the more you cut, the larger the plant will grow.

Culture. Oregano likes full sun; my plants have done well in average well-drained garden soil.

Uses. A culinary herb, it is used in many Italian dishes.

Remarks. The *majorana* is, in my opinion, mistakenly called sweet marjoram. The two herbs have similar fragrances, but marjoram is a tender herb, and *majorana,* much larger, is hardy in South Texas.

Oregano grows well in a planter box and is a classic for cookery.

PARSLEY
(Petroselinum hortense [crispum]) B

Propagation: Seed

Width & Height: 2' × 1'

Soil: Average

Exposure: Full sun or partial shade

Water: Average

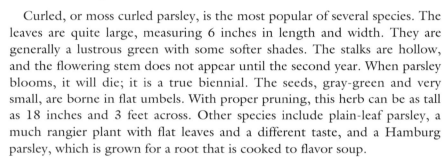

Curled, or moss curled parsley, is the most popular of several species. The leaves are quite large, measuring 6 inches in length and width. They are generally a lustrous green with some softer shades. The stalks are hollow, and the flowering stem does not appear until the second year. When parsley blooms, it will die; it is a true biennial. The seeds, gray-green and very small, are borne in flat umbels. With proper pruning, this herb can be as tall as 18 inches and 3 feet across. Other species include plain-leaf parsley, a much rangier plant with flat leaves and a different taste, and a Hamburg parsley, which is grown for a root that is cooked to flavor soup.

Culture. Parsley likes a moist, well-drained soil; my plants do best when some shade is provided. I plant them close to taller plants.

Uses. Parsley leaves garnish almost all meat dishes, can be used on and in salads, and give a nice flavor to soup. A medicinal tea is prepared from the dried leaves.

Remarks. Curled parsley makes a fine border plant along the walk or driveway. In most of the South, several plantings of parsley can be made during the year. Store in freezer.

PENNYROYAL (Mentha pulegium) P

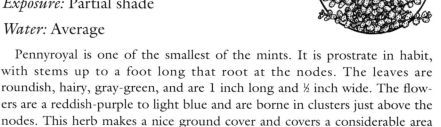

Propagation: Seed, cuttings, or plant division

Width & Height: 2′ × .1′

Soil: Average

Exposure: Partial shade

Water: Average

Pennyroyal is one of the smallest of the mints. It is prostrate in habit, with stems up to a foot long that root at the nodes. The leaves are roundish, hairy, gray-green, and are 1 inch long and ½ inch wide. The flowers are a reddish-purple to light blue and are borne in clusters just above the nodes. This herb makes a nice ground cover and covers a considerable area in a growing season.

Culture. My pennyroyal does well in partial shade in sandy soil, with a little extra water every now and then.

Uses. It is used in infusions to promote perspiration. A handful of the leaves rubbed into the coat of your dog or cat will repel fleas.

Remarks. This herb needs winter protection in zone 9. I pile a leaf and grass mulch around my beds, and, when a frost is predicted, completely cover my pennyroyal. I uncover it the next day, saving my mulch for the next frost.

PYRETHRUM (Chrysanthemum cinerariaefolium) P

Propagation: Seed or root division

Width & Height: 1′ × 2′

Soil: Sandy

Exposure: Full sun

Water: Average

This herb reaches 2 feet tall, with beautiful white, crimson, or pink daisy-like flowers. (Daisy is a member of this genus.) The plant can be cut back to bloom again. The leaves are dark green and finely cut.

Culture. Pyrethrum needs full sun and sandy, friable, moderately rich soil. Its seed is difficult to germinate; use sterile soil and propagate indoors. It's easier to grow from root division in early spring.

Uses. An organic insecticide powder is derived from the flowers of this herb. It is effective against many harmful vegetable insects and is harmless to warm-blooded mammals (you and me). An insect repellent is also prepared that can be used on exposed skin to keep away insects.

Remarks. This is a difficult herb to get started, but one well worth it. Plant 30 percent more plants than you'd like to have. For no apparent reason, hale and hardy plants expire.

ROSE (Rosa gallica officinalis) P

Propagation: Cuttings

Width & Height: 3' × 3'

Soil: Sandy with good drainage

Exposure: Full sun

Water: Average

Culture. Roses require excellent drainage (raised beds), in a sunny location, for optimum growth. They like good, rich soil, slightly acidic (pH 6.5), and regular fertilization (about four times a year) such as 12-24-12. Give them plenty of water, and mulch year-round to protect in winter and to hold water and moisture in summer. For more details on rose culture, see *A Garden Book for Houston and the Gulf Coast,* fourth edition, Gulf Publishing Company, Houston.

Uses. Though we usually plant roses for the decorative value of their flowers, the plants are also grown for the distillation of their essential oil and for the medicinal value of rose hips. The distillate is used to make rose water, a refreshing drink, or fragrant finger bowl. The essence, of course, is also used in perfumes.

Rose hip tea, rich in vitamin C, is fairly simple to make. Gather the hips after the first frost, when they will be slightly soft to the touch. Crush them with a pestle or rolling pin (avoid using a metal utensil, for this will discolor the rose hips and oxidize the vitamin C), and soak 4 tablespoons of crushed hips in 5 pints of water for 24 hours. Afterwards, simmer gently for ½ hour, but don't boil. Strain and store in tinted bottles or earthenware jars. Sweeten with honey when ready to use.

ROSEMARY (Rosemarinus officinalis) P

Propagaion: Seed or cuttings

Width & Height: 2' × 3'

Soil: Average

Exposure: Full sun or partial shade

Water: Average

The evergreen leaves of this shrub-like herb are an inch long, dark green on top and a lighter green on the underside. The light blue flowers are very small and bloom through most of the summer. This species is about 4 feet tall and 2 to 3 feet wide. I prefer *R. prostratus,* which is a low-growing species and makes an excellent low hedge. Prostrate rosemary is almost bonsai in appearance, with its woody twisted branches. This variety is a foot tall and 2 to 3 feet wide. The leaves are very similar to *R. officinalis* (upright rosemary), but not quite as long or wide. Leaves of both species have a piney odor. This is a very fragrant herb. There are a least a dozen varieties of this herb.

Culture. Does well in any well-drained soil and can manage on minimum water. It does best in full sun but can tolerate some shade during the day.

Uses. Rosemary is an excellent culinary herb for flavoring many meat dishes. Oil of rosemary has been used for relief of headaches. It is an ingredient in hair lotions and has been used as a rinse for the prevention of dandruff. It is a common ingredient in colognes.

Rosemary has small light blue flowers that bloom through most of the summer.

Remarks. A lovely herb for the garden or a container. Rosemary won't get as large grown indoors, but it will do very well.

Spanish legend has it that the Virgin Mary, while journeying to Egypt, draped her cloak over a bush of white-blooming rosemary. When she removed her cloak from the bush, the blooms had taken on the blue color of her garment.

Rosemary is also known as the herb of remembrance. Centuries ago this herb was used for happy occasions such as weddings, festivals, and banquets. Sorcerers and witches say it is useful in casting spells. *R. officinalis* (upright) is more cold–hardy than prostrate rosemary.

RUE (Ruta graveolnes) P

Propagation: Seed, cuttings, or root
  division

Width & Height: 1' × 2'

Soil: Sandy

Exposure: Full sun

Water: Minimum

This hardy, shrubby, evergreen, a native of southern Europe, reaches a height of 2 feet and perhaps a foot wide. The leaves are blue-green, and can reach 5 inches in length and half as wide. The flowers are a bright yellow, button-like, and ½ inch wide. The entire plant has a strong and, in my opinion, disagreeable odor. The taste is best described in one word—ugh!

Culture. Rue does best in poor, dry sandy soil in full sun. I read that rue and basil should not be planted together, so, as an experiment, I planted them side by side. The sweet herb, basil, overpowered the malodorous one, and the rue expired in about four weeks. Basil must release a chemical or exude a gas that kills rue.

Showy yellow flowers of rue make it an attractive border or hedge. Don't plant near basil.

Uses. Italians and Greeks use rue in salads. It is also used in some perfumes.

Remarks. Go easy on fertilizing rue. It is excellent as a low hedge or border plant along a walk or driveway.

SAGE (Salvia officinalis) P

Propagation: Seed and cuttings

Width & Height: 2' × 3'

Soil: Sandy

Exposure: Full sun

Water: Minimum

    This herb can reach 3 feet in height and width. The leaves, depending on the species, can range from 3 to 6 inches in length and half as wide. The leaves are finely wrinkled and gray-green in color. The purple flowers are in whorls. The stem becomes quite woody before the plant reaches full maturity. There are many varieties of sage, i.e., red, golden, narrow-leaf, variegated, and several others. In addition to the common, I grow variegated and golden, two very striking plants.

Golden sage.

Variegated sage.

Culture. All species like sandy, well-drained soil in full sun. I suggest a 6- to 8-inch hill to plant your sage, and no matter what the average rainfall is in your particular zone, don't water after your plant reaches maturity. You can fertilize lightly after pruning. Sage is hardy in all zones.

Uses. Sage is used to flavor many foods. It is also used to flavor wines, and a tea is made from the leaves. A gargle can be made from the leaves, and dried leaves can be smoked like tobacco.

Remarks. As with many of the herbs, the ancient herbalists ascribed magical properties to sage. According to them, sage, too, is great for the venomous bites of serpents.

(Pineapple) SAGE
(Salvia rutalins) P

Propagation: Cuttings

Width & Height: 3' × 4'

Soil: Average

Exposure: Full sun or partial shade

Water: Average

The semi-woody stems of pineapple sage can grow over 4 feet tall, and the entire plant can get as wide as 6 feet. The leaves, a medium to light green, are 2 to 3 inches long and up to 2 inches wide. The rough, pointed leaves, with a delicious pineapple fragrance, decrease in size and increase in number as they approach the terminus of the stem. The flowers, up to 2 inches long, are deep red and appear in early summer.

Culture. This plant does well in any garden soil and has a tendency to wilt when it needs water. If you notice wilting, a good watering will take care of it.

Uses. The fragrant leaves are excellent for potpourri and are used to flavor cold drinks.

Remarks. In our long growing season, pineapple sage can get to be quite large. Allow for adequate space. I suggest planting it in the background of your garden.

SANTOLINA
(Santolina chamaecyparissus) P

Propagation: Cuttings

Width & Height: 3' × 1'

Soil: Sandy

Exposure: Full sun

Water: Minimum

This gray, woody shrub is 2 feet tall and wide. The gray leaves are very small and form a dense coral-like mound. The flowers are clustered yellow buttons that appear late in summer. Both leaves and flowers have a pungent odor. Lavender, cotton, or gray santolina are other common names. Another species, *S. vireus,* is about the same size, but the foliage is green and not as dense as the gray. The flowers of green santolina are a green-yellowish color. Both santolinas have an almost menthol fragrance.

Culture. Santolinas thrive in full hot sun, in sandy, well-drained soil with minimum watering.

Uses. The oils have been used to treat ringworm, and the leaves and twigs are a moth deterrent amongst your woolens. The oils are also used in the manufacture of some perfumes.

Remarks. A beautiful edge plant as a low hedge; I insist that you secure a few of each species for your yard.

SASSAFRAS (Sassafras albidum) P

Propagation: Seed and cuttings

Width & Height: 8' × 30'

Soil: Average

Exposure: Full sun or partial shade

Water: Average

This North American tree can reach 100 feet in height, though I've never seen one that tall. Most get to 20 or 30 feet. The leaves are downy on the underside and vary in shape from ovate to elliptic, entire or three-lobed. The lobed leaf looks like a mitten. The flowers are small, yellow, and inconspicuous.

Culture. Sassafras does best in sandy, acid soil with a fair amount of sun. Try to find trees that are native to your area. If you live in zone 9, don't send off to a nursery in zone 3; you may have problems adapting that particular tree to your backyard.

Uses. The oil distilled from the rootbark is used in the manufacture of perfumes and soap. The wood and bark furnish a yellow dye. Tea is made from the roots, and young shoots and leaves are used to thicken gumbo.

Remarks. Everyone should have a sassafras tree. The fall color of the leaves is absolutely lovely.

SAVORY (Satureja hortensis) A

Propagation: Seed

Width & Height: ½' × 2'

Soil: Average

Exposure: Full sun

Water: Average

Summer savory is a hardy annual with slender stems that reach up to 16 inches tall. The flowers are very small, like the medium green leaves, and are a light lilac color. The stems become quite woody, and the entire plant has an almost windblown appearance. Winter savory, *S. montana,* is a perennial and is quite different in appearance. It's usually 2 to 3 feet across and a foot tall. The small leaves are dark green, shiny, and arranged in opposite pairs on the stem. The white flowers are less than a ¼ inch across with several on a cluster. Both herbs have a very pleasant spicy scent.

Culture. Both summer and winter savory like sandy well-drained soil but will do well in any soil. They can manage with minimum water. Summer seedlings transplant very well.

Uses. Summer savory is the preferred condiment, and the leaves are used to flavor salads, meats, beans, and other foods. It's a good plant for bees.

Remarks. This is one of my wife's favorite herbs, and because she's my favorite, it's one of mine. Winter savory makes a nice low hedge, requiring minimum care.

SHALLOTS (Allium cepa ascalonicum) P

Propagation: By individual cloves or
  bulbs

Width & Height: 1' × 3'

Soil: Average

Exposure: Full sun

Water: Average

I grow the Louisiana shallot (Delta Giant), which does well in all zones.
The mature plant will reach 3 to 4 feet tall, and a clump can reach 18 inches

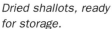

*Dried shallots, ready
for storage.*

in width. The hollow, cylindrical leaves are very similar to chives but are much larger. Shallots flower in mid-summer in ball-shaped clusters of white seed heads 3 inches wide.

Culture. Shallots like rich, well-drained soil and do best in full sun.

Uses. A highly prized culinary herb for meat, soups, stews, and many other foods. Young shallots can be eaten like green onions. Shallots are a bit stronger than chives but have a more delicate flavor than onions.

Remarks. I have grown shallots from bulbs I purchased in the northeast. They were a brownskin variety and didn't do too well in my garden. I prefer the Louisiana shallot.

It takes approximately 6 months for shallots to bulb up. To tell when they are ready, just brush the soil away from the top of the clump. You can pull the shallots up after a few months growth, prune off the tops, separate into bulbs (or cloves), and replant. They need to bulb-up before they can be stored. When they're bulbed-up, pull the entire plant up, wash off the soil, and hang in open shade with good air circulation. A clean, hot attic or garage is a good place. In 3 to 4 weeks, the tops should dry and fall off and the bulbs can be stored in a cool place.

SORREL (Rumex acetosa) P

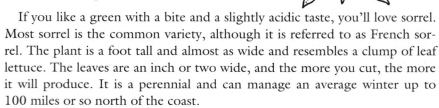

Propagation: Seeds

Width & Height: 6″ × 18″

Soil: Average

Exposure: Full sun

Water: Average

If you like a green with a bite and a slightly acidic taste, you'll love sorrel. Most sorrel is the common variety, although it is referred to as French sorrel. The plant is a foot tall and almost as wide and resembles a clump of leaf lettuce. The leaves are an inch or two wide, and the more you cut, the more it will produce. It is a perennial and can manage an average winter up to 100 miles or so north of the coast.

The flowers are reddish and should be pruned when they appear. This will extend the availability of good, tasty leaves.

Culture. Hardy in most zones.

Uses. In salads and the prime ingredient in sorrel soup.

Remarks. This plant is found in Europe, Asia, North America, and even in Greenland. The tangy flavor of the leaves apparently is appreciated more by the French. I have grown this herb in past years. It has lost its popularity here, but perhaps it will come back again.

SOUTHERNWOOD (Artemisia abrotanum) P

Propagation: Seed, cuttings, or plant division

Width & Height: 2′ × 3′

Soil: Average

Exposure: Full sun or partial shade

Water: Minimum

This feathery gray-green plant, or small shrub, is 18 inches tall and 3 to 4 feet across. It is an interesting specimen, with a bonsai appearance. The leaves are finely divided and give the plant a delicate, graceful look. My plants haven't flowered, but I've seen southernwood outside the South with yellowish-white flowers.

Culture. This plant does well in poor soil in full or partial sun.

Uses. Southernwood is used as a culinary herb in Italy. It is also used, in conjunction with other dried herbs, as a moth repellent for stored woolens.

Remarks. According to Culpeper, Dioscorides said it was good for worms in children. Years ago in Europe, a sprig of southernwood was included in a bouquet the young men gave to their girls.

The lacy foliage of southernwood.

SWEET FLAG (Acorus calamus) P

Propagation: Root division

Width & Height: 5′ × 10′

Soil: Average

Exposure: Full sun or partial shade

Water: Average

This native plant has long slender, lily-like leaves that get as tall as 6 feet. The yellow-green leaves, approximately ¾ inch wide, rise from a sheath. A flower stalk projects at a slight angle to the leaves, and the 3-inch cone-shaped spadix is covered with minute yellowish-green flowers. The leaves and root have a strong lemon scent. As the root gets drier, its scent becomes stronger.

Culture. This hardy perennial thrives in full sun in moist soil, but it will do well under fairly dry conditions.

Uses. Pieces of root are used as protection from household insects that attack books and furs. The candied roots are used for coughs and colds in Europe. The leaves are used as flavoring for custards and puddings. The English use oil extracted from the root bark to flavor beer.

Remarks. In fields and along the marshes this plant reaches 6 feet. In your garden it may reach 3 feet. Sweet flag is an interesting and unusual plant.

TANSY (Tanacetum vulgare) P

Propagation: Seed or plant division

Width & Height: 2′ × 3′

Soil: Average

Exposure: Full sun or partial shade

Water: Average

This herb can reach 3 feet in height and almost as wide. The fern-like leaves, dark green and sharply cut, are 6 inches long and about 4 inches wide. The yellow flowers grow in round, dull button-like clusters. The stems die down every year and reappear in the spring. There are several varieties of tansy.

Culture. Tansy thrives in most well-drained soils in full or partial sun.

Uses. Tansy oil is used in some perfumes. This herb has been used to treat some skin diseases. If taken internally in large doses, it can be harmful.

The dark green, fern-like leaves of tansy are a fly-repellant.

Remarks. The origin of the name is thought to be derived from the Greek *Athanaton* (immortal) because the flowers last for a long time. Tansy leaves also deter flies. It is said that if the leaves are rubbed on spoiled meat, it'll keep the flies off.

TARRAGON
(Artemisia dracunculus) P

Propagation: By root division in early spring

Width & Height: 1' × 2'

Soil: Sandy

Exposure: Partial shade

Water: Average

   This perennial grows to a height of 2 feet and 1½ feet wide, with 3-inch long, narrow dark green leaves. Tarragon rarely blossoms; when it does, it is late in summer, with small round yellow flowers dashed with black. Tarragon is a rather floppy looking plant and looks almost as though it has permanent wilt. There are two varieties of tarragon: French (*A. dracunculus*)

French tarragon: a naturally drooping plant and a culinary staple.

and Russian (*A. redowski*). Russian is propagated by seed, root division, and cuttings, and is very similar in appearance to French, though Russian tarragon's leaves are a lighter green. Russian tarragon has absolutely no flavor. It tastes like Bermuda grass.

Culture. Both varieties like full sun, sandy soil, and minimum fertilizing. French tarragon is very difficult to grow in the hot summer of most zones. It will do best in the northeast portion of zone 7.

Uses. Tarragon is used as a culinary herb for flavoring many types of salads; it's also excellent in vinegar.

Remarks. The name tarragon is a corruption of the French *Esdragon,* derived from the Latin *dracunculus* (little dragon), by which it is sometimes called.

THYME (Thymus vulgare) P

Propagation: By seed or cuttings

Width & Height: 2' × 1'

Soil: Sandy

Exposure: Full sun

Water: Minimum

   This hardy perennial, English thyme, reaches a height of 1 foot and a width of 2 feet. The gray-green leaves are ¼ inch long, slightly wider at the base, and slightly hairy. The stems and roots become quite woody in a brief growing period. The light pink flowers are in conical spikes at the ends of the branches; they'll bloom twice if the plant is pruned after its initial flowering.

Culture. *T. vulgare* is hardy in all zones; the other varieties are hardy in zone 9 but need winter protection in zone 8. Thyme does best in full sun in most any soil with minimum water. If thyme is grown

Creeping golden thyme, a beautiful ground or rock cover, has numerous culinary uses. Bees love it, too.

with only a few hours of sun, the leaves will be light green and the stalks tend to droop.

Uses. Thyme's principal use is for flavoring. Oil is extracted and used in colognes and soaps.

Remarks. There are many varieties of thyme. French thyme has a narrower, lighter green leaf but botanically is still considered *T. vulgare*. Mother of thyme (*T. sergyllum*) is an excellent rock garden herb. This ground cover plant makes a lovely carpet in one growing season. If you want to cover a large area, plants should be set out on 12-inch diagonals. There is golden lemon thyme (*T. citrodorus aures*) with golden leaves. *T. nutmeg,* another mat-forming thyme, has purple flowers. There are also a pine-scented thyme, marjoram wooly thyme, and several others.

This is an excellent herb for bees. Honey flavored with thyme commands a higher retail price than other honey. Mother of thyme (*T. serpyllum*) grows wild in Europe, and bee hives are set out to take advantage of the herb's nectar.

VIOLET (Viola odorata) P

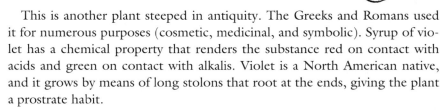

Propagation: Cuttings, root division

Soil: Rich, humus

Exposure: Full sun best

Water: Minimum

This is another plant steeped in antiquity. The Greeks and Romans used it for numerous purposes (cosmetic, medicinal, and symbolic). Syrup of violet has a chemical property that renders the substance red on contact with acids and green on contact with alkalis. Violet is a North American native, and it grows by means of long stolons that root at the ends, giving the plant a prostrate habit.

Culture. It can tolerate dry soil and is winter hardy in zones 7, 8, and 9. Violet does best in rich soil, in a sunny location. Propagate from seed, division, or cuttings. The easiest way is to plant runners (divisions) in spring or fall, in friable, humus-enriched soil. Remove dead leaves before planting, and keep the plants moist for the first few weeks. This is a lovely border or accent plant.

Uses. You can press the flowers and spray them with a solution of gum arabic, sugar, and water to make candied violets. After spraying, dry in the oven at 100°. Be sure you store them in an airtight container to retard deterioration or invasion by roaches and other ugly bugs.

Remark. The Greeks called it Ione, because Io, a princess loved by Jupiter, was changed by him into a heifer to protect her from Juno. Gee whiz!

WATERCRESS
(Nasturtuim officinals) P

Propagation: Cuttings

Width & Height: ½″ × 3″–4″

Soil: Water or very moist growing medium

Exposure: Fair amount of sun

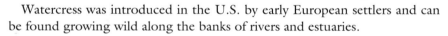

Watercress was introduced in the U.S. by early European settlers and can be found growing wild along the banks of rivers and estuaries.

Culture. Since it is a nydrophyte (growing with roots submerged in water or very moist soil), you'll have to grow it in gravel beds or beds of very sandy soil, with a constant source of slow-running water.

Watercress is usually propagated by inserting a cutting of a plant in the growing medium on an angle complementary with the direction of the current. The plants will root quickly, and you can harvest as soon as healthy, lush growth has begun.

Uses. High in vitamin C and iron, the herb is a classic in green salads. Its nutritive value is diminished by cooking, so always prepare it fresh. Watercress is also a good substitute for spinach, and it is delicious when chopped and minced with butter or your favorite sandwich spread.

WINTERGREEN
(Gaultheria procumbens) P

Propagation: Seed or plant division

Width & Height: 1' × 1'

Soil: Sandy

Exposure: Partial shade

Water: Minimum

Wintergreen is a native of North America and occurs as far south as Dallas. It is a low-growing shrub, usually less than a foot tall. The woody stems are covered with oval dark green leaves 1½ inches long and ½ inch wide. Young leaves are green with a slight yellow-red cast. The leaves have a peppermint fragrance. The berries, usually produced in late summer and early fall, have a pleasant taste.

Culture. Wintergreen likes partial shade and sandy, fairly rich soil.

Uses. Wintergreen oil was used to treat muscle aches and pains.

Remarks. Wintergreen can be grown in your yard, and it does best in the eastern portion of zones 7 and 8.

(Sweet) WOODRUFF
(Asperula odorata) P

Propagation: Plant division

Width & Height: 1' × 2'

Soil: Average

Exposure: Partial shade

Water: Average

This attractive plant is a lovely low-growing ground cover that spreads rapidly. The smooth stems reach 6 to 8 inches tall, and are covered with whorls of tiny white flowers. The yellow-green leaves are quite small and have a vanilla fragrance when crushed.

Culture. Sweet woodruff needs quite a bit of shade and will do best under trees or when shaded by tall plants. It requires more than average moisture and rich, friable, sandy soil.

Uses. The flowers are used in May wine or in hot tea.

Remarks. I have found sweet woodruff difficult to grow here in Houston. It's too hot along the coast, but it should do well in the eastern portions of zones 7 and 8.

WORMWOOD
(Artemisia absinthium) P

Propagation: Seed or cuttings

Width & Height: 2' × 2'

Soil: Average

Exposure: Full sun

Water: Minimum

Wormwood is probably the most familiar of the Artemisias. This herb reaches 4 feet in height and width. The leaves are a blue-gray and shaped somewhat like those of a chrysanthemum. The yellow flowers are very small and button-like. This is a very handsome plant, but it tends to get rank. Pruning your plant is necessary in late spring or early summer.

Culture. I found that wormwood does well in full sun and heavy soil.

Uses. It was used as an ingredient in conjunction with other herbs to treat gout. In France it was used to make absinthe, and it is now used in the manufacture of vermouth. Wormwood is one of the most bitter herbs.

Remarks. One variety, sagebrush (*A. tridenta*), a native of the American West, was a very useful herb for the Indians. It furnished dye for their cloth and is edible. I have seen sagebrush 12 feet tall.

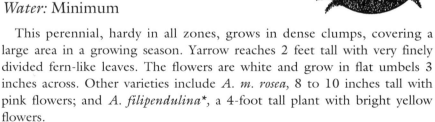

Wormwood, used in making absinthe and vermouth, has a very fresh, clean fragrance, but a rather bitter taste.

YARROW
(Achillea milleofolium) P

Propagation: Root division

Width & Height: 2' × 1'

Soil: Average

Exposure: Full sun

Water: Minimum

This perennial, hardy in all zones, grows in dense clumps, covering a large area in a growing season. Yarrow reaches 2 feet tall with very finely divided fern-like leaves. The flowers are white and grow in flat umbels 3 inches across. Other varieties include *A. m. rosea*, 8 to 10 inches tall with pink flowers; and *A. filipendulina**, a 4-foot tall plant with bright yellow flowers.

Yarrow flowers are white, pink, or yellow and grow in flat umbels.

Culture. Yarrow likes full sun, minimum moisture, and does well even in poor soil.

Uses. If you have any sick sheep, a tea made from yarrow is reputed to restore their health. Yarrow is used as a tea for colds, as a tonic, and as an ingredient in salads.

Remarks. A very easy herb to grow, the fern-like leaves are excellent with flower arrangements. When the leaf dries it retains the original leaf pattern.

Herbs from Around the World

....

Agrimony *(Agrimonia eupatoria):* This native of Britain is commonly used to flavor tea and wine, having a flavor reminiscent of the apricot. Unlike most herbs, agrimony is harvested when in flower (usually in late May or June). The flowers are produced in elongated yellow spires, and when grown amidst other herbs, agrimony will give your garden a pleasant, wild look.

It is tolerant of a wide range of soils and situations, but always provide good drainage, a reasonable amount of sun, and some organic matter to enrich the soil.

Arugula, Rugula, Roquette Riquette, Garden Rocket *(Eruca vesicara):* Seeds can be sown all year long in south Texas. Arugula is hardy to about the mid-20s. The dark green leaves can almost be mistaken for oak leaf lettuce. During the cooler months the plant reaches 2 feet in height and width. In the hot months, it is perhaps half as large. Never let arugula go to seed. Prune off the seed heads to prolong the life of the plant.

For the summer growing season, plant seeds every few weeks for a constant supply. Italy and France are probably the origin of this plant, and friends who have visited there tell me it's all over the countryside.

Arugula's nutty flavor goes great with a dollop of goat cheese and sliced tomatoes. It's a love/hate affair; either you love arugula or you hate it. Some restaurants mix it with other greens such as lettuce or radicchio.

Seeds are available as Garden Rocket from Nichols. (See Sources).

179

Epazote *(Chenopodium ambrosioides):* A native of Mexico, this plant reaches up to 3 feet tall and 4 feet wide. The long narrow serrated leaves are about 3 inches long and an inch wide. They have an almost camphor smell, which is far removed from a fragrance.

In hot weather, the plant goes to seed, but the foliage can be extended by pruning. Once you've planted epazote, it will drop seeds and it can take over a growing area. I know it does well ±100 miles north of the Houston area and grows well in and around Austin.

It is said (by whom I don't know) that cooking black beans and adding epazote will eliminate the aftereffects—not true. Seeds are available from Shepards (See Sources).

Fennugreek *(Trigonella faenum-graecum):* This is one of the most ancient plants in cultivation. The Egyptians used it as a constituent of embalming oil; today it is the principle source of an extract used in imitation maple syrup, as well as an ingredient in many spice blends, such as curry powder. It tolerates a wide variety of conditions, but prefers a fairly dry soil. The plant can be grown from seed (which germinates quickly after sowing) or from cuttings. Fennugreek is thought to aid in the production of diosgenin, a compound used to produce steroidal hormones such as progesterone, and so may have future use in contraceptive treatments.

Gentian *(Gentiana lutea):* According to the Greek, Dioscorides, this medicinal plant was first put to use by Gentius, King of Illyria, from 180–167 B.C., who extracted the bitter juice from the root. Gentian is a rather slow-growing, long-lived plant (up to 50 years), and its huge spongy root extends as deep as 3 feet into the soil. It likes a slightly alkaline, preferably calcareous, rich clay soil. Fall is the best time to harvest the roots, for that is when they are richest in gentian-in, the bitter medicinal substance.

Gentian can be grown from seed germinated indoors and transplanted, or you can purchase starter plants. Remember—once you situate the plant, you'll have to leave it there because of its deep root.

Ho Ra Pa *(Cinnamon Basil):* According to my Thai friends—and I have several—this herb is Thai in origin. The plant is about 1½ feet by 1½ feet, and leaves are 1½ inches long and half as wide. As the name implies, they have a strong fragrance. The seed heads are a lovely light purple in color, and they are very attractive plants for your herb garden. I'm not much of a cook. Wait a minute! I'm not a cook, but people I know mix some of these leaves with sweet basil for Pesto.

Jasmine *(Jasminum officinale):* This is a gracious addition to any garden. This native of the Near and Middle East is highly valued for perfumery. Jasmine grows as a woody, flowering vine and makes an excellent ground cover or border planting. Average fertilizer and moisture are suitable, and it can take either full sun or partial shade. Propagate by layering or from cuttings; prune in the fall, after flowering.

Kah Prow *(Thai Basil):* I don't know if this is a true basil. I have tried to get my Thai friends to find the Latin name—no such luck.

In full sun the upper two-thirds of this 2 feet by 2 feet plant are reddish-purple, the lower third green. Leaves are small, about an inch long and half as wide and add a slight bite to food they are used to flavor. Many Thai dishes are flavored with this herb, and seeds are available at Nichols Nursery (See Sources) or contact your local nursery for live plants.

Makrut, Makrood *(Citrus Hystrix):* I found out recently, after growing this Thai citrus for several years, that it is also called Keifer lime. In a very large pot, 20-gallon size or so, the plant can reach 10 feet tall. The green, very shiny leaves grow as doubles, one an extension of the other. The thorns are over an inch long, and care must be taken around this plant. The leaves have a wonderful citrus fragrance, and sliced thin, are used in many Thai dishes. Don't pick individual leaves to use, but rather a cutting with a few leaves. The latter method induces more growth.

This is a very tender citrus and must be protected in cold weather.

Ohja Santa *(Piper auritum):* This semi-woody plant dies back in the winter and, like magic, reappears in the spring. It manages quite well along the coast and north to Austin. I sent some plants out to Portland, Oregon and they didn't make it. But then it gets below zero there. It is a multiplier and in a few growing seasons can cover a large area. Leaves reach up to 16 inches long and half as wide. The more you cut, the more it reproduces.

My wife uses it to wrap and bake fish, fowl, and pork chops. Chefs I know chop it up and use these sarsaparilla-flavored leaves with other greens in salads.

This Mexican herb came to me from my dear friend Lucinda Hutson, author of *The Herb Gardening Cook Book* (available from Gulf Publishing Company). She has some wonderful recipes for Mexican and Thai herbs.

Prrk *(Thai Pepper):* Here is a small, thin 1- to 2-inch hot pepper, and I DO MEAN HOT. The plant can reach 4 feet in height and width. The peppers are green, turn almost black, then red, and regardless of color, are hot. It is used to flavor several of the spicy Thai dishes. Panang, like a curry, is my favorite.

The Herbs at a Glance

Herb	Plant Habit (A = annual, B = biennial, P = perennial)	Light: Full Sun	Light: Partial Shade	Water: Min.	Water: Avg.	Water: Freq.	Soil: Avg.	Soil: Sandy	Dimensions Width & Height (feet)	Evergreen Zone(s)	Propagation (S = seeds, C = cuttings, D = plant or root division)	Plantings: Hang. Basket	Plantings: Does Well Indoors	Plantings: Ground Cover	Teas	Remarks
Aloe	P	X	X		X			X	1 × 2	9, 10	†		X			Good for skin irritations
Angelica	P		X		X	X	X		2 × 5	9, 10	S					Plant in background
Anise	A	X			X		X		1 × 2	—	S		X			Plant with coriander
Basil	A	X			X			X	2 × 2	—	S, C	X				Very easy to grow
Bay	P	X	X	X	X		X		5 × 10	9, 10	S, C					Pot plant in zones 7 and 8
Bee Balm	P	X			X		X		2 × 3	8, 10	S, C				X	Pretty flowers
Borage	A	X	X		X		X		1 × 2	—	S					Beautiful flowers
Camomile (English)	P	X	X		X	X		X	2 × 2½	9, 10	S, C, D			X	X	Lovely, fragrant mat
Camomile (German)	A	X	X		X	X		X	½ × 1	—	S					Pretty daisy-like flowers
Caraway	B	X			X		X		1 × 3	8, 9, 10	S		X			Unusual seed head
Catnip	P	X	X		X		X		3 × 2	9, 10	S, C, D				X	Gets scraggly—prune
Cayenne	P	X	X		X		X		1 × 2	10	S					Hot! Grown as annual
Chervil	A		X		X			X	1 × 2	—	S		X			Lacy light green leaves used like parsley
Chives	P	X	X		X		X		½ × 1	All	S, D	X	X			Great culinary herb
Comfrey	P	X			X		X		2 × 3	9, 10	D				X	Plant off in the corner
Coriander	A	X			X		X		1 × 2	—	S					Plant with anise
Costmary	P	X	X		X		X		1 × 2	All	D				X	Unusual mint fragrance
Dill	A	X			X		X		1 × 3	—	S					For pickling
Dittany of Crete	P	X		X				X	1 × 2	9, 10	S, C	X	X	X		Great for hanging basket
Elecampane	P		X		X			X	2 × 4	9, 10	S, D				X	Large daisy-like flower
Fennel (Florence)	A	X			X		X		1 × 2	—	S					Eat stalks like celery

The Herbs at a Glance (Continued)

Herb	Plant Habit (A = annual, B = biennial, P = perennial)	Light Full Sun	Light Partial Shade	Water Min.	Water Avg.	Water Freq.	Soil Avg.	Soil Sandy	Dimensions Width & Height (feet)	Evergreen Zone(s)	Propagation (S = seeds, C = cuttings, D = plant or root division)	Plantings Hang. Basket	Plantings Does Well Indoors	Plantings Ground Cover	Teas	Remarks
Fennel	P	X			X		X		2 × 4	9, 10	S				X	Big herb: seeds used for flavoring Italian sausage, cordials, liqueurs.
Foxglove	B	X				X	X		1 × 4	9, 10	S					Beautiful flowers, showy; yields digitalis, a heart stimulant.
Garlic	P	X			X		X		1 × 3	—	D					Random plant
Garlic Chives	P	X	X		X		X		½ × 1	9, 10	D	X				A must for salads
Germander	P	X		X			X		1½ × 1	All	C		X			Beautiful flowering hedge
Ginger	P	X			X		X		1 × 2	10	D					Lovely fragrance
Ginseng	P		X		X		X		1 × 1½	—	S			X		Tough to grow
Horehound	P	X		X			X		6 × 1½	9, 10	S, C				X	Gets scraggly—
Horseradish	P	X			X		X		1 × 2	—	D					Dig up every bit of root
Hyssop	P	X		X				X	1 × 1	All	S, C, D				X	Lovely low hedge plant
Lambs Ear	P	X		X				X	1 × 1	9, 10	S, D					Soft, furry leaves
Lavender	P	X		X				X	1 × 2	8, 9, 10	S, C					Plant in raised beds; flowers have exquisite fragrance
Lemon Balm	P	X	X	X			X		1 × 3	8, 9, 10	S, C, D	X	X		X	Gets scraggly
Lemon Grass	P	X			X		X		1 × 2	9, 10	D				X	Excellent tea
Lemon Tree	P	X			X		X		3 × 10	9, 10	S, C					Lovely Eucalyptus
Lemon Verbena	P	X			X		X		2 × 4	9, 10	S, C	X	X		X	Pungent lemon fragrance
Luffa	A	X			X		X		15 × 3	8, 9, 10	S					Excellent body sponges
Marjoram	A	X			X		X		3 × 1	9, 10	S, C	X	X			Very pretty plant; culinary herb
Mexican Marigold																
Mint	P	X			X		X		1 × 2	9, 10	S, C, D	X	X		X	Licorice fragrance
Mint Spp.	P	X			X	X	X		3 × 1	9, 10	S, C, D	X	X		X	Great for teas
Mint, Corsican	P		X		X	X	X		3 × .1	9, 10	S, C, D	X				Only an inch tall
Mugwort	P	X			X		X		3 × 2	8, 9, 10	S, C	X			X	British used it for tea

The Herbs at a Glance (Continued)

Herb	Plant Habit (A=annual, B=biennial, P=perennial)	Light: Full Sun	Light: Partial Shade	Water: Min.	Water: Avg.	Water: Freq.	Soil: Avg.	Soil: Sandy	Dimensions Width & Height (feet)	Evergreen Zone(s)	Propagation (S=seeds, C=cuttings, D=plant or root division)	Plantings: Hang. Basket	Plantings: Does Well Indoors	Plantings: Ground Cover	Teas	Remarks
Nasturtium	P	X			X			X	1 × 2	10	S		X			Grown as an annual
Oregano	P	X	X		X		X		1 × 2	8, 9, 10	S, C, D		X			Great for Italian foods
Oregano (Majorana)	P	X	X		X		X		4 × 1	10	S, C	X				Great for many foods
Oregano (Greek)	P	X	X		X		X		2 × 1	9, 10	S, C, D	X	X			Makes an interesting Bonsai
Parsley, moss	B	X	X		X		X		2 × 1	8, 9, 10	S	X	X			Good border plant
Parsley, flat leaf	B	X	X		X		X		2 × 2	8, 9, 10	S		X			Best parsley
Pennyroyal	P		X		X		X		2 × .1	9, 10	S, C, D	X		X	X	1 inch tall
Pineapple Sage	P	X	X		X		X		3 × 4	9, 10	C	X			X	Delicious fragrance; good background plant
Pyrethrum	P	X			X			X	1 × 2	9, 10	S			X		Organic insecticide powder
Rose	P	X			X			X	3 × 3		C				X	Rose hip tea
Rosemary (Upright)	P	X	X		X		X		2 × 3	8, 9, 10	S		X		X	Excellent culinary or decorative herb
Rosemary (Prostrate)	P	X	X		X		X		1 × 2	8, 9, 10	S	X	X		X	Excellent culinary or decorative herb
Rue	P	X		X				X	1 × 2	8, 9, 10	S, C, D		X			Don't plant near basil
Sage	P	X		X				X	2 × 3	All	S, C	X	X		X	Needs good drainage; plant on mounds or in raised beds
Salad Burnet	P	X			X		X		2 × 2	All	S, D		X		X	Cucumber flavored leaf
Santolina	P	X		X				X	3 × 1	All	C		X			For low hedge
Sassafras	P	X	X		X		X		8 × 30	—	S, C				X	A lovely tree
Savory, Summer	A	X			X		X		½ × 1	—	S		X			A fine culinary herb
Savory, Winter	P	X			X		X		3 × 1	8, 9, 10	S, C		X			Low hedge

The Herbs at a Glance (Continued)

Herb	Plant Habit A = annual B = biennial P = perennial	Light Full Sun	Light Partial Shade	Water Min.	Water Avg.	Water Freq.	Soil Avg.	Soil Sandy	Dimensions Width & Height (feet)	Evergreen Zone(s)	Propagation S = seeds C = cuttings D = plant or root division	Plantings Hang. Basket	Plantings Does Well Indoors	Plantings Ground Cover	Teas	Remarks
Scent, Geraniums	P	X	X	X				X	½ × 1	10	S, C	**	X			Delicious fragrances
Shallots	P	X			X		X		1 × 3	—	D					Random plant
Sorrel	P	X			X		X		½ × 1½	—	S					A green with a bite
Southernwood	P	X	X	X			X		2 × 3	All	S, C, D					Does well in any soil
Sweet Flag	P	X				X	X		1 × 6	8, 9, 10	D					Fine lemon fragrance
Sweet Woodruff	P		X		X		X		1 × 2	9, 10	D			X		Beautiful ground cover
Tansy	P	X	X		X		X		2 × 3	9, 10	S, D					Pretty herb; inedible; deters flies
Tarragon (French)	P		X					X	1 × 2	9, 10	D	X	X			Naturally wilted appearance; minimal fertilizer
Tarragon (Russian)	P	X	X						1 × 2	9, 10	S, C	X	X			Easy to grow along the coast
Thyme	P	X		X				X	2 × 1	All	S, C	X	X			Very hardy plant; plant near bee hives for flavored honey
Violet	P	X		X			X		½" × 4"	7, 8, 9	S, D, C					Pretty flowers
Watercress	P	X				X		X			C					High in Vitamin C and iron
Wintergreen	P		X	X				X	1 × 1	All	S, D				X	A nice bush: pleasant mint taste
Wormwood	P	X		X			X		2 × 2	8, 9, 10	S, C					A graceful plant; once used to make absinthe
Yarrow	P	X		X			X		2 × 1	9, 10	D				X	Dried leaves hold shape, good in floral arrangements

*I've estimated on some of the northern limits of evergreen zones and have included zones in which I am confident they will be evergreen. It may well be that in some cases they are evergreen another zone north. The criteria for evergreen zone(s) is average mean temperature, and an unusually cold winter can change some of the classifications.

† Aloe—Propagation by vegetative offshoots from the mother plant.

**Scented Geraniums; coconut, apple, and nutmeg for hanging baskets.

In the Vernacular . . .

English	Botanical Name	French	German	Spanish	Italian
agrimony	*Agrimonia eupatoria*	agrimoine soubeirette	kleiner Odermennig	agrimonia	agrimonia
angelica	*Angelica archangelica*	angélique	Angelika Engelwurz	angélica	angelica
basil	*Ocimum basilicum*	basilic	Basilienkraut	albahaca alabega	basilico
bay	*Laurus nobilis*	baie	Lorbeer	laurel	lauro
bee balm	*Monarda didyma*	bergamote	Bergamotten- baum	bergamota bergamoto	bergamotta
borage	*Borago officinalis*	bourrache	Borretsch	borraja	borragina borrana
burnet	*Sanguisorba* spp.	pimprenelle	Pimpernell	pimpinella	pimpinella
caraway	*Carum carvi*	carvi	Kümmel	alcaravea carvi	carvi
catnip	*Nepeta cataria*	herbe aux chats cataire	Katzenminze	menta de gato	nepeta erba dei gatti
camomile	*Anthemis nobilis*	camomille romaine	Kamille	manzanilla camomila	camomila
chervil	*Anthriscus cerefolium*	cerfeuil	Kerbel	perifollo	cerfoglio
chicory	*Cichorium intybus*	chicorée	Zichorie	achicoris	cicoria
chives	*Allium schoenoprasum*	ciboulette	Schnittlauch	cebollino cebolleta	cipollina
comfrey	*Symphytum officinale*	consoude	Schwarzurz	consuelda	consolida
coriander	*Coriandrum sativum*	coriandre	Koriander	cilantro	coriandolo
costmary	*Tanecetum balsamita* (syn. *Chrysan- themum balsamita*)	herbe Sainte- Marie tanaisle balsamite	Alecost		tanaceto balsamatico
dill	*Anethum graveolens*	aneth fenouil bâtard fenouil puant	Dill	eneldo	anito
elecampane	*Inula helenium*	aunée	Alant Alantwurzel	énula	enula campana
fennel	*Foeniculum officinale*	fenouil	Fenchel Schwarzkümmel	hinojo	finocchio
fenugreek	*Trigonella foenum- graecum*	fénugrec	Bockshornklee	alhoula	fieno greco
foxglove	*Digitalis purpurea*	digitale	Fingerhut	digitalis dedalera	digitale
garlic	*Allium sativum*	ails	Knoblauch	ajo	aglio
gentian	*Gentiana lutea*	gentiane	Enzian	genciana	genziana
geranium	*Geranium* spp.	géranium	Storchschnabel	geranio	geranio
horehound, black	*Ballota nigra*	marrube noir	schwarze Bulte		marrubio nero
horehound, white	*marrubium vulgare*	marrube blanc	weisse Andorn	marrubio	marrubio comune
horseradish	*Cochlearia rusticana*	raifort	Meerettich	rábano picante o rústico	rafano
hyssop	*Hyssopus officinalis*	hysope	Ysop	hisopo	issopo
jasmine	*Jasminum officinale*	jasmine	Jasmin	jazmin	gelsomino
lavender	*Lavendula officinalis*	lavande spic	Lavendel	lavándula espliego	lavanda spiganardo
lemon balm	*Melissa officinalis*	mélisse	Melisse	balsamita	balsamo
lemon verbena	*Lippia citriodora*	citronnelle	Eisenkraut	verbena	berbena

(table continued on next page)

In the Vernacular . . . (Continued)

English	Botanical Name	French	German	Spanish	Italian
marigold	*Calendula officinalis*	souci	Dotterblume Ringelblume	cálendula flamenquilla	calendula fiorrancia
marjoram (sweet)	*Marjorana hortensis*	marjolaine	Marjoran	megorana	maggiorana
mint	*Mentha* spp.	menthe	Minze	menta	menta
mullein	*Verbascum thapsus*	molène bouillon blanc	Wollkraut	verbasco gordolobo	verbasco
nasturtium	*Tropaeolum majus*	capucine	Kapuzinerkresse	capuchina nasturcia	nasturzio
onion	*Allium* spp.	oignon	Zwiebel	cebolla	cipolla
oregano	*Origanum* spp.	origam	Majoram	oregano	oregano
parsley	*Petroselinum crispum*	persil	Petersilie	perejil	prezzemolo
pelargonium	*Pelargonium* spp.	pelargonium	Pelargonie	pelargonio	pelargonio
pyrethrum	*Pyrethrum coccineum*	pyrèthre	Pyrethrum	piretro	piretro
rhubarb	*Rheum officinale*	rhubarbe	Rhabarber		rubarbaro
rose	*Rosa* spp.	rose églantier odorant	Rose wilde Rose	rosa escarmujo olorosso agavanzo	rosa rosa selvatica
rosemary	*Rosmarinus officinalis*	romarin	Rosmarin	Rosmarino Romero	Rosmarino
English	Botanical Name	French	German	Spanish	Italian
rue	*Ruta graveolens*	rue	Raute	ruda trago amargo	ruta
saffron	*Crocus sativus*	safran	Safrangewürz	azafrando	zafferano
sage	*Salvia officinalis*	sauge	Salbei	salvia	salvia
santolina	*Santolina chamaecyparissus*	santoline	Buschzypress	santolina	santolina
savory	*Satureja* spp.	sarriette	Bohnenkraut	ajedrea	savore
tansy	*Tanacetum vulgare*	tanaisie herbe aux vers	Rainfarn Gänserich	tanaceto balsamita minor	tanaceto
tarragon	*Artemisia dracunculus*	estragon	Estragon	tarragón estragón	tarragone dragoncello
thyme	*Thumus* spp.	thym serpolet	Thymian	serpoleto tomillo	serpillo timo
violet	*Viola odorata*	violette	Veilchen	violeta	violetta mammola
wall germander	*Teucrium chamaedrys*	chéneau	Batenikel Berggamander	pinillo maro	germandria
watercress	*Nasturtium officinale*	cresson de fontaine	Brunnenkresse	berro	crescione di fonte
wintergreen	*Gaultheria procumbens*	gauthérie couchée	Wintergrün		tè di montagne
woodruff, sweet	*Asperula odorata*	aspérule odorante	Waldmeier		raspello odoroso
wormwood	*Artemisia* spp.	absinthe armoise	Absinth	alcachofa arcacil	carciofo
yarrow	*Achillea millefolium*	millefeuilles herbe aux charpentiers	Schafgarbe	milenrama	millefoglie

Sources

....

When you order herb plants, have them sent by air rather than surface mail. They'll arrive in a few days and in good condition.

Richter's Herb Seed Catalog ($1.00)
Goodwood, Ontario LOC IAO

   One of the largest listings of herb seeds.

J. L. Hudson, Seedsman ($1.00 for catalog)
P.O. Box 1058
Redwood City, CA 94064

   Their catalog is a fascinating little book listing many varieties of herb seeds. It also lists seeds of rare and unusual plants, shrubs, and trees.

Nichols Garden Nursery (Free catalog)
1190 North Pacific Highway
Albany, Oregon 97321

   An excellent selection of herb plants and seeds. They carry seeds of unusual vegetables from around the world, including some from the People's Republic of China, Japan, Italy, France, and other countries.

Park Seed (Free catalog)
Greenwood, South Carolina 29647-0001

   Seed for some of the scented geraniums and many different herbs.

Burpee Seed (Free catalog)
Clinton, Iowa 52732

   Many varieties of herb seeds and plants.

Shepards Garden Seed
6116 Highway 9
Felton, CA 95018

A good seed selection that includes epazote and Thai peppers.

Graingers

Check telephone directory for store nearest your home. Solenoid valves and time clocks are available from their catalog.

Local nurseries with a good selection of herb plants and seeds include:

Cornelius Nurseries, Inc.
2233 S. Voss Rd.
Houston, TX
782-8640

and three other Houston locations.

Teas Nursery Co., Inc.
4400 Bellaire Blvd.
Bellaire, TX
664-4400

Index

About the Author

Sol Meltzer grows and sells herbs from his garden. He wrote a monthly garden column for *The Houston Gardener* and *Houston City Magazine,* has done many radio and television shows on herbs and organic gardening, taught courses on herbs and organic gardening, and is a guest lecturer to garden clubs throughout Texas. By profession, he is a petroleum geologist (retired), formerly with Cities Service Oil Co.

Mr. Meltzer grows almost every herb he has written about. He supplies several chefs with the fresh culinary herbs they use in their entrees. He also supplies health food stores, nurseries, plant shops, and other retail outlets with potted herb plants. He and Thelma, his wife, live in Houston, Texas.